NuWave Oven Cookbook

250 Amazingly Easy Recipes to Fry, Bake, Grill and Roast with Your Nuwave Oven

By

Amanda Graves

Copyright © 2018 by Amanda Graves. All Right Reserved.

No part of this publication may be reproduced, distributed, or transmitted in any form or by any means, including photocopying, recording, or other electronic or mechanical methods, or by any information storage and retrieval system without the prior written permission of the publisher, except in the case of very brief quotations embodied in critical reviews and certain other noncommercial uses permitted by copyright law.

TABLE OF CONTENTS

Introduction 1

Benefits of NuWave Oven 2

Tips and Tricks for Cooking with Your Nuwave Oven 4

NuWave Oven Temperature Conversion Guide 5

Conversions Chart 6

BREAKFAST RECIPES 7

    1. Cheese and Pasta Frittata 7

    2. Steak Stuffed Tomatoes and Cheese Eggs 7

    3. Delicious Cinnamon Twists 8

    4. Chopped Bacon Omelets 8

    5. Corn Syrup and Brown Sugar French Toast 9

    6. Sausage and Egg Breakfast Pudding 9

    7. Cranberry Scones 10

    8. Delicious Milky Brunch Bread Pudding 11

    9. Succulent Cheesy Asparagus Frittatas 12

    10. Pecan Streusel and Blueberry Cake 13

    11. Vegemite Scrolls and Cheese 13

    12. Tasty Mini Crustless Quiche 14

    13. Pecan and Maple Syrup Cinnamon Rolls 14

    14. Amazingly Stuffed Banana French Toast 15

    15. Delicious Brekkie Muffins 15

    16. Quick and Easy Steak & Eggs with Cheese Stuffed Tomatoes 16

    17. Delicious Pizza with Tomato sauce 16

    18. Spinach Havarti Frittata 17

    19. Corn and Bacon Pizza 18

    20. Egg with Manchego 18

    21. Amazing Breakfast Bikkies 18

    22. Tasty Baked Eggs with Cherry Tomatoes and Spinach 19

    23. Easy Crunchy French Toast 19

24. Smoked Salmon Quesadilla with Cream Chives and Cheese 20

SNACKS & APPETIZERS 21

25. Delicious Cheesy Mixed Vegetable Quesadillas 21
26. Toasted Bacon and Grilled Cheese, Apple Sandwiches 21
27. Delicious Cheese Stuffed Mushroom Caps 22
28. Sour Cream and Ranch Stuff Potato Bites 22
29. Goat Cheese and Walnut, Pear Crostini 22
30. Tasty Garlic Buttermilk Biscuit Bread Bites 23
31. Tasty Herb Cheese Fries 24
32. Caramel Glaze Chicken Skewers 25
33. Toasted Pita Chips with Garlic and Artichoke Dip 26
34. Fried Ravioli 26
35. Delicious Triple Cheese Garlic Bread 27
36. Spicy and Sweet Roasted Nuts 27
37. Amazing Bacon Wrapped Shrimp Bites 28
38. Tasty Corn and Jalapeño Cheddar, Muffins 28
39. Tasty NuWave Nachos 29
40. Corn, Zucchini and Black Bean Quesadillas 29
41. Garlic Bread 30
42. Succulent Italian Bread Loaf Pizza 30
43. Yummy Cheesy Bacon and Tater Tot Bombs 31
44. Amazing Beefy Bacon Wrapped Tater Tots 31
45. Delicious Cereal Party Mix 32
46. Cheesy Nachos 32
47. Apple Jelly Glazed Chicken Wings 33
48. Orleans Style Crab Cakes 33
49. Jalapeno and Cheddar Muffins 34
50. Chicken, Asparagus and Corn Tarts 35
51. Nuwave Style Pesto Stars 35
52. Nuwave Style Hommus 35
53. Tasty Crunchy Sausage Rolls 36

54. Vegetable and Chicken Pies 36

55. Delicious Pesto 37

56. Nuwave Style Chilli Con Carne 37

57. Tasty Pita Crisps 37

58. Cheese, Bacon & Corn Muffins 38

59. Amazing Mexican Bagels 38

60. Delicious Curry Puffs 39

61. Cashew and Capsicum Pesto 39

62. Delicious Savory Muffins 40

63. Amazing Chicken, Tarragon and Leek Pie 40

POULTRY RECIPES 42

64. Delicious Crispy Honey Crusted and Ginger Chicken 42

65. Tasty Spicy & Sweet BBQ Chicken 42

66. Cheese Filled Crunchy Chicken 43

67. Italian style Rubbed Turkey 43

68. Cheesy Turkey Burgers 44

69. Roasted Chicken and Onions 44

70. Creamy Chicken Breasts with Bell Peppers and Mushrooms 45

71. Delicious Chicken Parmesan 45

72. Cilantro and Lime Chicken 46

73. Tasty Fried Chicken 46

74. Tasty Chicken Parmesan 47

75. Delicious Grilled Cilantro and Garlic Chicken Breasts 48

76. Amazing Almond, Chicken and Bacon Filled Croissants 49

77. Tasty Corn, Chicken and Cheese Enchiladas 49

78. Special Turkey Burgers 50

79. Grilled Cornish Game Hens with Potatoes and Artichokes 51

80. Hot & Spicy Chicken Curry 51

81. Quick & Easy BBQ Chicken 52

82. Thai Chicken With Assorted Vegetables 52

83. Roasted Chicken In BBQ Sauce 53

84. Hot & Delicious Buffalo Chicken Hoagie Roll Sandwiches...53
85. Easy Cheese, Chicken and Spinach Pasta Bake...54
86. Tasty Turkey and Apple Meatloaves...55
87. Stuffed Roasted Chicken Breast..55
88. Chicken Bites with Wasabi Mayonnaise Dipping Sauce..56
89. Fresh Turkey Dish..56
90. Amazing Roasted Dijon and Herb Encrusted Chicken Breast..57
91. Tasty Italian Style Chicken...58
92. Yummy Chicken Wraps..58
93. Cheering Chicken in Amazing Alfredo Sauce Rolls...59
94. Chicken Nugget Casserole...60

BEEF & LAMB RECIPES...61

95. Amazingly Easy Cottage Pie..61
96. Delicious and Cheesy Beef Burgers..61
97. Delicious Ancho Chili Spiced Lamb Burgers...62
98. Lamb Chops with a Mint and Red Pepper Sauce..63
99. Delicious Andouille & Beef Burgers with Spicy Mayonnaise and Caramelized Onions......63
100. Tasty Beef Wellingtons..64
101. Chuck Roast Beef With Roasted Potatoes..65
102. Tasty Sausages with Bacon and Prunes..66
103. Delicious Veggie and Meat Tortilla Rolls...66
104. Speedy Lamb Meatballs..67
105. Roasted Lamb Chops..67
106. Rosemary and Lamb Cottage Pie...68
107. Barbeque Lamb Skewers..68
108. Jack O' Peppers...69
109. Mustard Coated Leg of Lamb..69
110. Yummy Cheesy Meatloaf..70
111. Feta and Tomato Topped Grilled Lamb Chops..71
112. Delicious Mustard and Thyme Crusted Lamb..71
113. Spicy Louisiana Sliders with a Mustard Remoulade Sauce......................................72

- 114. Herb Butter Stuffed Lamb Chops 73
- 115. Quick and Easy Rib Roast 74
- 116. Bacon, Liver & Onions 74
- 117. Lamb Burgers With Orange and Olive Salsa 75
- 118. Delicious Bacon Wrapped Meatloaf 75
- 119. Shepherd's Pie 76
- 120. Rosemary, Thyme Crusted Lamb Shanks 77
- 121. Tangy Thai Steak, Peanut Salad and Bean Sprout 77
- 122. Stuffed Cabbage Rolls 78
- 123. Tarragon and Butter Stuffed Lamb Chops 79
- 124. Sour and Sweet Lamb Chops 79
- 125. Tasty Steak Sandwiches 79
- 126. Crabmeat Stuffed Beef Roulade 80
- 127. Easy Rib Eye Steak 82

SEAFOODS RECIPES 83

- 128. Easy Creamy Tuna Mornay 83
- 129. Tangy Lemon Salmon Topped With a Sweet and Spicy Mango Salsa ... 83
- 130. Delicious Soy Salmon 84
- 131. Easy Nutty Orange Chili Salmon 84
- 132. Quick and Easy Garlic Prawn Rolls 85
- 133. Delicious Baked Lobster Tail With Bacon Mornay 85
- 134. Funny Taco Chicken Strips 86
- 135. Delicious Filo Wrapped Salmon With Greek Yoghurt And Dill Dressing .. 86
- 136. Zingy Roasted Shrimp with a Herbed Salsa 86
- 137. A Medley of Shellfish 87
- 138. Mouth Watering Curried Prawns 87
- 139. Delicious Potato Topped Tilapia Fillets with A Herbed Sour Cream 88
- 140. Mouthwatering Moroccan Fish Skewers 89
- 141. Perfect Salmon Pie 89
- 142. Tasty Tuna and Sweetcorn Potatoes 90
- 143. Amazing Parmesan Topped Scallops 90

144. Simple Tuna Steaks with a Tangy Orange Salsa ... 91
145. Zesty Salmon With Fennel and Lemon ... 91
146. Thai Style Chili Snapper ... 92
147. Tuna and Noodle Casserole ... 92
148. Hot & Zingy Clams & Sausage ... 93
149. Healthy Asparagus and Pesto Topped Orange Roughy ... 94
150. NuWave Style Quick N Easy Lobster Thermidor ... 94
151. Cheesy Crab Dip with Toasted Wonton Wrappers ... 95
152. Grilled Halibut with a Tangy Clementine Gremolata ... 95
153. Oven Grilled Salmon ... 96
154. Oven Fried Catfish ... 96
155. Special Oven Grilled Tuna Steaks ... 97
156. Fennel Coated Bass ... 97
157. Spicy Red Snapper with Red Onion and Orange ... 98
158. Tasty Oven Grilled Shrimp In Chipotle Sauce ... 98
159. Baked Shrimp ... 99
160. Tasty Tuna Noodle Casserole ... 99

VEGETARIAN RECIPES ... 100

161. Cheesy Zucchini and Onion Au Gratin ... 100
162. Creamy Baked Sweet Potatoes ... 100
163. Herbed Winter Vegetables ... 101
164. Delicious Feta and Artichoke Tortilla Wraps with a Chive and Yogurt Dip ... 101
165. Crunchy French Beans with Almond Topped ... 102
166. Spicy Grilled Vegetables with a Yogurt and Tahini Dip ... 102
167. Streusel Topped Buttery Sweet Potato Casserole ... 103
168. Classical Stuffed Capsicums ... 104
169. Tofu, Cheese and Marinara Sauce Stuffed Bell Peppers ... 104
170. Roasted Chickpeas, Cauliflower and Olives ... 105
171. Delicious Ricotta and Spinach Stuffer Lasagna Rolls ... 105
172. Roasted Cauliflower, Olives and Chickpeas ... 106
173. Parmesan Crusted Asparagus Spears with Balsamic Vinegar ... 106

- 174. Roasted Mushrooms 107
- 175. Delicious Mayonnaise & Cheese Covered Corn 107
- 176. Roasted Garlic Mushrooms 107
- 177. Spicy Roasted Corn and Zucchini 108
- 178. Chive Topped Potatoes 108
- 179. Ricotta and Spinach Stuffed Jumbo Pasta Shells 109
- 180. Crust less Quiche - Mushroom and Bacon 109
- 181. Roasted Russet Potatoes 110
- 182. Baked Tomato and Cheese Casserole 110
- 183. Herbed Fingerling Potatoes 111
- 184. Vegetables Stuffed Mushrooms 111
- 185. Quick and Easy Roasted Butternut Squash 112
- 186. Pinto Bean Burgers 112
- 187. Easy Cheesy Quesadillas 113
- 188. Cauliflower and Broccoli Gratin 113
- 189. Butter Hassel back Potatoes 114

DESSERTS & PUDDINGS 115

- 190. Greek Style Lemon Yoghurt Syrup Cake 115
- 191. Pumpkin Cookie Sandwiches with a Cream Cheese Filling 115
- 192. Kids Favorite Chocolate Cake 116
- 193. Tasty Lemon Meringue Pie 117
- 194. Tasty Cherry Galette 118
- 195. Cranberry and Apple Turnovers 118
- 196. Polenta Syrup and Orange Cake 119
- 197. Fruit Kebabs With Orange Sauce and Passionfruit 120
- 198. Sweet Hot Cross Bun Pudding 120
- 199. Delicious Profiteroles 121
- 200. Amazingly Easy Two-Egg Pavlova 122
- 201. Blueberry Muffins 122
- 202. Delicious Cinnamon Apple Filo Pastries 123
- 203. My Favorite Plum Tart 123

204. Popular Portuguese Custard Tarts 124
205. Granny Smith Apple Sponge Pudding 124
206. Nuwave Style Queen Puddings 125
207. Delicious Classic Pavlova 125
208. Amazing Bourbon, Caramel Pudding 126
209. Nuwave Style Baked Rice Puddings 126
210. Mouthwatering Hummingbird Muffins With Creamed Honey Spread ... 127
211. Orange Glazed Carrot Cake 127
212. Lemon and Poppy Seed Glazed Cookies 128
213. Delicious Chocolate Topped Oat Cookies 129
214. Delicious Dense Pound Cake 130
215. Butter and Bread Pudding 130
216. Nuwave Style Baked Filled Peach Halves 131
217. Chocolate Cake (Egg less) 131
218. Honey and Cinnamon Crackers 132
219. Chocolate Chip Oatmeal Cookies 132
220. Easy Plum Crumbles 133
221. Banana Pineapple Nut Bread 134
222. Salted Chocolate Tart 134
223. Coconut and Raspberry Muffins 135
224. Mix Berry Cream Pie 136
225. Easy Banana Puddings 136
226. Orange Crinkle Cookies 137
227. Lemon Candy Topped Iced Cookies 138
228. NuWave Chocolate Cake 139
229. Maraschino Cherry Stuffed Cherry Glazed Cookies 139
230. Yummy Apple Crisp 140
231. Lemon Cookies Topped With Lemon Candies 141
232. Raspberry Crumble 142
233. Tasty Carrot Cake Cookies 142
234. Tasty Banana Bread 143

235. Chocolate Tart 143

236. Oatmeal Cookie Cake 144

237. Pear Custard Pie 145

238. Delicious Jam Biscuits and Almond 145

239. Amazing Scones 146

240. Easy Honey Cornbread 146

241. Coconut Slice and Raspberry 147

242. Ginger Anzac and Macadamia Biscuits 147

243. Cheesecake Cookies 148

244. Tasty Salted Chocolate Tart 148

245. Tasty Butter Biscuits 149

246. Stuffed Baked Apples 150

247. Halloween Special Pumpkin Cheesecake 150

248. Maple Glazed Dense Pound Cake 151

249. Egg-Less Arrowroot Biscuits 152

250. Orange and Buttermilk Cupcakes 153

Introduction

This famous multi-purpose counter top kitchen appliance comes with the combination of 3 styles of heat - convection, conduction and infrared. This special combination will save a whole lot of time and energy, while trimming the extra fats and calories from your foods.

Whenever you prepare food in the NuWave oven, it's not necessary to pre-heat it nor do you need to defrost foods before putting it inside the oven. Take away the frozen foods from the refrigerator and directly pop them into NuWave oven. Set the time & heat and relax while your NuWave oven does all of the hard work!

The NuWave oven also uses a 'layered cooking' model for added convenience. Which means that you can actually prepare multiple items inside your NuWave oven simultaneously, without their flavors mixing up or even mingling with each other. Therefore, you can make a vegetarian food and also a nonvegetarian food together, without any of the flavours spoiling the taste of the separated dishes.

Whenever you cook food in your NuWave oven, you are building a healthy choice. Simply because you no longer need to use any kind of extra fat while cooking food in a NuWave oven. That is right; absolutely no additional butter or oil required to do any of the cooking. Additionally, if you are using fat rich meats or your marinade has a healthy quantity of fat in it, really do not worry! The special design of the NuWave oven ensures that all of the extra fat from your food is drained and all you get it succulent and healthy low-fat foods! Because of its 3-heat technology, vegetables not only cook quicker, but also retain a substantial amount of the nutritional value present in them which is generally lost when you cook vegetables in the normal oven!

Benefits of NuWave Oven

NuWave Oven is really a new method of cooking. This oven uses 3 different types of heat production together, that is convection, infrared and conduction so that you can prepare food more effectively. Below are some of the benefits of using a NuWave Oven.

Healthy and Delicious Cooking:

The NuWave oven, as discussed before, works with a triple combination cooking power to cook foods. This powerful cooking method removes all of the extra fat from your food, in the form of fat drippings, although food remains juicy and tender on the inside

Additionally, with a faster cooking cycle, the NuWave oven makes sure that the nutritional value within your food is not lost because of heating for several hours. Therefore, when it is all said and done, you have healthy meals on your plate which is low on fat but is incredibly juicy and it has the majority of its nutrients undamaged

Seafood & Meats Come out Completely Delicious:

You can actually cook many different food items in the NuWave oven, from vegetables to poultry to meat to sea food of all types, however regular users recognize that the best use for NuWave oven is to cook several tasty meat or fish in it

Poultry including turkey and chicken can be cooked whole or even in some parts plus it turns out deliciously tender and succulent with a perfectly golden brownish exterior. Fish cooked in the NuWave oven has a perfectly flaky interior along with the crispy exterior

Great Time Saver:

One of the greatest features of the NuWave oven is that it is a real time saver. It's not necessary to pre-heat it in advance. This will save you a great 20 mins (that you may have spent watching for your oven to reach the correct temperature) and you can simply turn on, place your food in and it will be cooked immediately!

One more essential time saver is that by cooking frozen food items all the way through, they do not need to be defrosted. Yes, you read that right. You don't need to defrost your frozen foods to room temp before you cook them. Remove frozen foods from the fridge, put it in your NuWave oven, set the temperature that's it! your tasty food will be ready immediately.

Re-heat Just like a Pro:

Imagine if I tell you that this NuWave oven will not just simply re-heat your food, but breathe a new life into it? Think about, re-heating a pizza without having its crust getting hard and the entire pizza getting chewy. Re-heat some refrigerated fried chicken breast leftovers and keep a look as its extra fat drips away, leaving you with a fat free and crispy chicken so that you can eat and appreciate.

Power Saver:

Usually when you use the NuWave oven, not only you are saving time and making some tasty meals, but you are also doing your little bit in order to save our planet. How? Read on to learn! While using NuWave oven instead of your regular oven will save you a lot of energy

A whopping 2/3 of the energy that you would normally be used to operate your conventional oven is used by the NuWave oven. Simply because will not waste any energy pre-heating your oven. If you use a conventional oven, you need to pre-heat it, so that it can be able to achieve the suitable temperature

Tips and Tricks for Cooking with Your Nuwave Oven

1. Do you know that you can't simply bake and grill in your NuWave oven, but you can also toast several different breads, bagels or English muffins inside it? Place the selection of breads on the 4-inch rack on high and you will have completely toasted bread within Four mins

2. When you deal with your NuWave oven, during or after cooking, make sure that you always have your oven mitts on. You may not feel the heat radiating off it immediately, however your NuWave oven is hot and can scald your palms and fingers terribly if you are not careful.

3. While using multi-level cooking function on the NuWave oven is actually both fun and very easy! Everything you need to keep in mind is that all the foods usually do not take the same amount of time to get perfectly cooked. Therefore, the foods which take longer to cook, for example meats, needs to be placed in the oven on the lower racks and once they're almost done, faster cooking food items must be placed on the higher racks

4. It is important that you clean your NuWave oven after each use. If you don't clean after every use, the leftovers from the previous cook may end up burning and sticking with your oven, making the clean up afterwards an even bigger head ache.

5. After grilling your preferred meats, cleaning up the fat droppings can be an absolute pain. To help you to cleanup easier and head ache free, place a piece of heavy-duty aluminium foil on the Linear Pan. Once you have finished cooking, you can simply lift the foil from the Linear Pan and get rid of it without having to scrub the pan!

6. Prior to removing the power head from NuWave oven, make sure that the dome of the oven has cooled down completely.

7. Whenever you clean your NuWave oven, make sure that the oven is turned off, cooled and also unplugged before you start

8. Don't use rough pads or chemical cleaners while cleaning NuWave oven. They may damage the surface of your oven. It is also recommended that you don't put any of the enamel racks in the dishwasher and you should always clean all of them manually

NuWave Oven Temperature Conversion Guide

Oven Temperature in Fahrenheit	Oven Temperature in Celsius	Power Level
106 degrees Fahrenheit.	41 degrees Celsius.	1
116 degrees Fahrenheit.	47 degrees Celsius.	2
150 degrees Fahrenheit.	66 degrees Celsius.	3
175 degrees Fahrenheit.	79 degrees Celsius.	4
225 degrees Fahrenheit.	107 degrees Celsius.	5
250 degrees Fahrenheit.	121 degrees Celsius.	6
275 degrees Fahrenheit.	135 degrees Celsius.	7
300 degrees Fahrenheit.	149 degrees Celsius.	8
325 degrees Fahrenheit.	163 degrees Celsius.	9
342 degrees Fahrenheit.	172 degrees Celsius.	10 (HI)

Conversions Chart

UNIT:	EQUALS:	ALSO EQUALS:
1 teaspoon	1/3 tablespoon	1/6 fluid ounce
1 tablespoon	3 teaspoons	1/2 fluid ounce
1/8 cup	2 tablespoons	1 fluid ounce
1/4 cup	4 tablespoons	2 fluid ounces
1/3 cup	1/4 cup plus 4 teaspoons	2 ¾ fluid ounces
1/2 cup	8 tablespoons	4 fluid ounces
1 cup	1/2 pint	8 fluid ounces
1 pint	2 cups	16 fluid ounces
1 quart	4 cups	32 fluid ounces
1 liter	1 quart plus ¼ cup	4 ¼ cups
1 gallon	4 quarts	16 cups

BREAKFAST RECIPES

1. Cheese and Pasta Frittata

Ingredients:

- 1/6 cup ricotta
- 2 large eggs
- ½-cup grated parmesan cheese
- 8 slices bacon
- ½ tablespoon olive oil
- ¼-cup tomato sauce
- 1 ½-cups of pasta (any kind) spaghetti, linguine, macaroni, Orecchiette (cooked)

Instructions:

1. Place the bacon slices on a 4-inch cooking rack in a single layer. Cook on the HI setting for about 8 minutes.
2. Remove the bacon slices from the oven and cool before crumbling. You should have about ½-cup worth of crumbles.
3. Combine together the ricotta, eggs, Parmesan, bacon crumbles, olive oil, tomato sauce and pasta together in a large mixing bowl. Mix well until the pasta is well coated.
4. Lightly grease a large inch baking dish with some butter or spray with some cooking oil.
5. Pour the prepared pasta mix into the greased baking pan and use the back of a spoon or a spatula to press the mixture into the bottom of the pan.
6. Place the prepared baking pan on the 4-inch cooking rack and bake for about 12 to 15 minutes or until the top gets a dark brown, crust like texture.
7. During the last 7 minutes of cooking, cover the baking pan with a foil to prevent over browning.
8. Place a serving plate over the baking pan upside down and flip the baking pan over. Lightly tap to de-mold. Serve hot.

2. Steak Stuffed Tomatoes and Cheese Eggs

Ingredients:

- 2 (4-ounce) sirloin steak
- 1 tomato; cut into halves and seeds removed
- Seasoned salt to taste
- 4 tablespoons Parmesan cheese; grated
- 4 large eggs
- 2 tablespoon butter
- 2 scallions; thinly sliced

Instructions:

1. Crack open the eggs in a shallow dish that is ovenproof.
2. Break the yolks carefully and place the dish on the liner pan.
3. Carefully slice the rounded side of the tomato halves a little so that they can stand on their bottom.
4. Stuff the tomato halves with the grated cheese.
5. Add the seasoned salt to the steaks and rub it in using your fingers.
6. Place the cheese stuffed tomato halves and the steak on the 3-inch rack.

7. Set you NuWave oven to the 'HI' setting and bake for about 9 to 10 minutes from a medium steak.
8. Cut the egg into two halves.
9. On two serving plates, place the steaks, cheese stuffed tomato halves and the eggs.
10. Serve immediately with some toasted bread.

3. Delicious Cinnamon Twists

Ingredients:
- 1 teaspoons cinnamon
- 1/2 cup sugar
- 1/2 (11-ounce) package frozen breadsticks

Instructions:
1. Combine the cinnamon and sugar in a medium sized mixing bowl. Whisk together using a wire whisk until well combined. Set aside.
2. Pour the cinnamon sugar into a flat plate.
3. Place a single breadstick in the cinnamon sugar mixture and roll until well coated.
4. Hold the breadstick from both ends in each hand and twist until you get a rope like texture.
5. Place on a 3-inch rack and bake on 'HI' for about 12 to 14 minutes, flipping it over at the halfway mark.
6. Serve with a side of apple sliced.

Note:
1. If you want softer and chewy twists; bake for about 7 to 9 minutes.
2. You can also brush the done cinnamon twisty with some melted butter and sprinkle some more cinnamon sugar on the twisty for some added flavor.
3. For a savory option; brush the breadstick with some egg and top with grated cheese, sesame seeds or some poppy seeds.

4. Chopped Bacon Omelets

Ingredients:
- 5 eggs
- 3 ounces Cheddar cheese; shredded
- 1/4 cup milk
- 1/2 cup beef bacon; chopped into bite sized pieces
- 1/8 cup onion; chopped
- 1/4 cup green pepper; chopped
- 1/2 tablespoon parsley

Instructions:
1. Place the eggs in a medium sized mixing bowl. Add in the milk and beat using a whisk until the eggs get a fluffy texture.
2. Add in the cheese, green pepper, beef bacon and onion and mix well.
3. Pour the egg and meat mixture in a 4-inch by 4-inch silicon baking dish (grease if you are using a normal baking dish).

4. Place the baking dish in on the 1-inch rack. Set the temperature on the 'HI' setting and bake for about 10 to 15 minutes.
5. Let the egg sit in the in the dome with the heat off for another minute.
6. Extract the egg from the silicon-baking dish and cut into pieces.
7. Serve hot with a side of baked English muffins or whole wheat bread.

Note: You can add any type of meat to the omelet, just chop it into bite-sized pieces and drain all the grease from it.

5. Corn Syrup and Brown Sugar French Toast

Ingredients:
- 1/8 cup butter
- ½ tablespoon corn syrup
- ¼-cup packed brown sugar
- 3 to 4 slices of (1-inch thick) bread; whole wheat or white
- 3/8 cup milk or half and half
- 2 large eggs
- 1/8 teaspoon salt
- ½ teaspoon vanilla

Instructions:
1. Heat a small sized saucepan over a medium flame.
2. Add in the butter and heat until melted.
3. Once the butter has liquefied, add in the corn syrup and brown sugar.
4. Continue heating until it gets a smooth consistency.
5. Pour the prepared mix into the bottom of an 8-inch by 8-inch baking pan or a round 10-inch baking pan.
6. Remove the crusts of the bread slices and place them in the bottom of the pan in a single layer. You may have to lightly flatten the bread slices so that they all fit easily in the pan.
7. Combine together the eggs, vanilla, salt, half and half or milk in a medium sized mixing bowl. Whisk well until all the ingredients are well incorporated.
8. Pour the prepared egg mixture over the bread slices.
9. Cover the pan and refrigerate for at least an hour, but it is preferred to let it rest overnight.
10. Place the prepared baking dish on the 1-inch cooking rack and bake on the HI power level for about 30 minutes.
11. If you feel that the top is browning too fast; cover the pan with some aluminum foil.
12. Serve warm with a side of fresh fruits.

6. Sausage and Egg Breakfast Pudding

Ingredients:
- 1 tablespoon olive oil
- 2 mushrooms; sliced
- ¼-cup leek; sliced
- 1 green onion; sliced
- 2 eggs
- 1 cup turkey breakfast sausage; large diced
- ½-cup heavy cream
- ½-cup Gouda cheese; shredded
- 3/8 cup milk

- 2 cups Hawaiian bread; diced into 1-inch cubes
- Freshly ground black pepper; to taste
- Kosher salt; to taste

Instructions:
1. Combine the olive oil, mushrooms, turkey sausage, leeks and onions together in a large 10-inch baking pan.
2. Sprinkle generous amounts of salt and pepper to season.
3. Place the prepared baking pan on the 3-inch cooking rack and cook for about 10 to 12 minutes at 300 degrees Fahrenheit. Stop the oven around the 5 to 6 minute mark and stir well to ensure even cooking.
4. While the sausage mixture is baking; place the eggs, milk, heavy cream and Gouda cheese together in a large mixing bowl. Whisk well until all the ingredients are well incorporated. Keep aside.
5. Once the sausage mix is done cooking; leave the baking pan in the oven to rest.
6. Place the bread cubes in the egg mixture and mix well until the bread is incorporated.
7. Remove the sausage mix from the oven and pour the prepared egg and bread mixture over the cooked sausage. Mix well until well combined.
8. Place the prepared baking pan on the 1-inch cooking rack and back for 50 to 55 minutes at 300 degrees Fahrenheit.
9. Bake until it gets a brown crust.
10. Once done; let the dish rest in the oven for a few minutes.
11. Serve hot topped with some fresh herbs or salsa of your choice.

7. Cranberry Scones

Servings: Serves 12

Ingredients:
- 4 cups all-purpose flour
- 2 tablespoon baking powder
- ½-cup packed brown sugar
- ½ teaspoon ground nutmeg
- ½-cup butter; chilled and diced
- ½ teaspoon salt
- 2 cups fresh cranberries; roughly chopped
- 2 grated zest of two oranges
- 2/3 cup white sugar
- 1 cup chopped walnuts
- 2 eggs
- 1 ½-cups half and half cream

Instructions:
1. Place the flour, baking powder, salt, brown sugar and nutmeg together in a large mixing bowl. Whisk using a wire whisk so that all the ingredients are well combined.
2. Add the butter to the bowl and mix well until the mixture resembles coarse sand. Keep aside.
3. In another bowl; mix the cranberries with the sugar and toss well until well coated.
4. Add the sugarcoated cranberries, walnuts and orange zest to the coarse flour -mix. Lightly mix until just combined. Keep aside.

5. In another mixing bowl place the cream and eggs together. Whisk well until the eggs are well incorporated.
6. Slowly pour the egg and cream mixture into the flour mix; mixing well after each addition.
7. Keep mixing until you form a soft dough.
8. Knead the dough with your hands about 5 to 6 times. Make sure you do not over knead it.
9. Divide the dough into four quarters
10. Place one quarter of the dough on a lightly floured workstation.
11. Roll the dough into a large circle; about 6 inches in diameter.
12. Cut the circle into 6 wedges.
13. Repeat with the remaining quarters until you have 24 wedges.
14. Rub some oil on the liner pan or spray it lightly with some cooking spray.
15. Place the Extender Ring on the base of your NuWave Oven Elite.
16. Place about 6 wedges around the perimeter of the prepared liner pan.
17. Bake for about 20 to 22 minutes at 300 degrees Fahrenheit.
18. Once the timer is up; remove the scones immediately from the oven and allow the scones to cool slightly before transferring to a cooling rack.
19. Repeat with the remaining wedges. And Serve warm.

8. Delicious Milky Brunch Bread Pudding

Ingredients:
- 1 tablespoons olive oil
- 2 mushrooms; sliced
- 1/4 cup leeks; sliced
- 1 green onions; sliced
- 2 eggs
- 1 cups turkey breakfast sausage; large diced
- 1/2 cup heavy cream
- 1/2 cup Gouda cheese; shredded
- 1/2 cup milk
- 2 cups Hawaiian bread; diced into 1-inch cubes
- Kosher salt; to taste
- Freshly ground black pepper; to taste

Instructions:
1. Combine the olive oil, mushrooms, sausage, leeks and onions together in a 10-inch ovenproof baking dish.
2. Season to taste with the kosher salt and freshly ground black pepper.
3. Place the baking dish on the 3-inch rack and cook on the '8' setting of your NuWave oven for about 10 minutes, pausing around the 5-minute mark to give it a stir.
4. While the mushroom and sausage mixture cooks; crack the eggs open in a large mixing bowl. Add in the Gouda, heavy cream and milk and whisk with a wire whisk until well combined. Keep aside.
5. Once the mushroom and sausage mix is cooked, place the cubes of bread in a separate bowl.
6. Pour the egg and milk mixture onto the bread cubes and mix well until well incorporated.
7. Pour the bread and egg mixture onto the cooked sausage and mushroom mixture. Mix well until well combined.

8. Place the baking pan on a 1-inch rack and bake on the '8' setting of your NuWave oven for 45 to 50 minutes or until set.
9. If the top starts browning too fast, cover the pan with a sheet of heavy-duty aluminum foil to ensure that the top does not burn while the insides cook.
10. Serve hot, topped with some fresh herbs or your favorite salsa.

9. *Succulent Cheesy Asparagus Frittatas*

Ingredients:
- 1/2 teaspoon butter
- 1/2 teaspoon chives; coarsely chopped
- 1 cup grated white Cheddar; divided into 1/4, 1/4 & 1/2
- 10 spears fresh asparagus; trimmed
- 1 small yellow onion; peeled and chopped
- 6 eggs; lightly beaten
- 1 small carrot; peeled, trimmed and finely grated
- 1/2 cup milk
- 1/2 cup self-rising flour
- 1/2 teaspoon salt
- 1/4 teaspoon freshly ground black pepper

Instructions:
1. Grease a 6-cup Bundt pan with some butter and keep aside.
2. Combine about 1/4 cup of the grated white Cheddar and 1/4 teaspoon chives together in a small bowl and keep aside.
3. Salt a large pot of water generously and heat over a high flame until bubbling. Lower the heat to a medium low and add in the asparagus spears.
4. Continue heating on a high flame for about 4 to 5 minutes or until the asparagus spears are tender.
5. Drain the asparagus spears from the water and place under cold running water for a few minutes until cool enough to handle.
6. Pat dry the asparagus spears using a kitchen towel; until dry.
7. Chop the asparagus spears into 1/4th-inch pieces and place the asparagus pieces in a large bowl.
8. Add in the remaining 1/4-cup of grated white Cheddar cheese, onions, flour, salt, eggs, carrots, milk and pepper to the bowl containing the asparagus and mix well.
9. Pour the prepared mix into the greased Bundt pan and place it on the 1-inch rack in your NuWave oven.
10. Bake on the 'HI' setting for 45 to 55 minutes or until firm.
11. Once done; allow the Bundt pan to cool until manageable and invert the frittatas onto a plate.
12. Sprinkle the remaining 1/2 cup grated white Cheddar cheese and the remaining 1/4 teaspoon chives on the frittatas.
13. Return the frittatas to the Bundt pan and place on the 1-inch rack.
14. Bake on the 'HI' setting for another 2 to 3 minutes or until the cheese melts.
15. Serve hot.

10. Pecan Streusel and Blueberry Cake

Ingredients for the cake:
- 1 cup fresh or frozen blueberries
- 2 cups and 3 tablespoons all-purpose flour
- 2 teaspoons baking powder
- 3/4 cup sugar
- 1/4 teaspoon salt
- 1/2 cup milk
- 1 egg
- 1/2 cup butter; softened
- 1 cup chopped pecans

Ingredients for the Streusel Topping:
- 1/3 cup all-purpose flour
- 1/4 cup cold butter
- 1/2 cup sugar

Instructions:
1. For the Streusel topping; combine the all-purpose flour and sugar together in a small mixing bowl.
2. Add in the butter and keep cutting in, until the mixture gets a crumbly – flakey texture.
3. Combine the all-purpose flour, baking powder, sugar and salt together in a large mixing bowl.
4. In a small mixing bowl combine the butter, milk and eggs together and whisk well until well combined.
5. Pour the wet ingredients into the dry ingredients and fold until it forms a smooth batter.
6. Lightly dust the blueberries and pecans in some icing sugar and add to the batter. Mix well until incorporated.
7. Grease a 9-inch spring form pan with some butter and dust with some flour.
8. Pour the prepared cake batter into the greased and dusted pan.
9. Top the cake batter with the prepared Streusel topping mix.
10. Place the extender ring on the base tray of your NuWave oven.
11. Place the spring form pan on the 1-inch rack and bake on the '8' setting for about 35 to 45 minutes or until a skewer poked into the center of the cake comes out clean.
12. Remove the pan from the oven and cool in the pan for 5 minutes.
13. Remove the cake from the oven and cool on a wire rack for another 10 minutes.
14. Slice and serve warm topped with some vanilla ice cream or a dollop of whipping cream.

11. Vegemite Scrolls and Cheese

Ingredients:
- 3 cups self-raising flour
- Pinch salt
- 1.8 oz. (50g) butter
- 375 ml milk
- 1 - 2 tablespoon vegemite
- 7 oz. (200g) tasty cheese; grated
- 2 tablespoon parmesan cheese (mix with tasty cheese)

Instructions:

1. Sift flour and salt into a bowl then rub through butter (alternatively, process flour & butter in food processor). Stir in enough milk to make soft dough. Knead gently on a lightly floured surface, and then roll to form a 40cm x 25cm rectangle.
2. Spread the Vegemite over the dough then sprinkle over 3/4 of the cheese. Roll up along the long side to enclose the cheese. Cut 10 x 4cm pieces from the roll and place close together, cut side up on baking paper on 5cm rack.
3. Sprinkle with the remaining cheese and bake in a NuWave oven for 10 minutes; turn over and bake a further 2mins.

Tips:
An even faster way to prepare these is to use frozen puff pastry which has been thawed for 10 minutes. spread with vegemite and cheese, roll up and cook as above.
Other variations you could try include: pizza scrolls, using cheese, capsicum and salami in a similar way sweet chilli and cheese capsicum chutney and cheese

12. Tasty Mini Crustless Quiche

Ingredients:
- 6 large eggs
- 1/2 cup whole milk
- 6 large egg yolks
- 1/2 cup heavy cream
- 1/2 teaspoon ground black pepper
- 1 teaspoon kosher salt
- 1-pound mixed bell peppers; seeded and diced

Instructions:
1. Crack the eggs into a large mixing bowl. Add in the egg yolks, cream, pepper, milk and salt to the bowl. Whisk well using a wire whisk until well combined and lightly fluffy.
2. Pour the egg mixture into a large glass jar or pitcher (or a cake batter dispenser if you have one!) and keep aside.
3. Place about 24 silicon mini cupcake liners (or 12 regular liners) on the rack. Spray them with cooking spray or lightly grease them.
4. Take about half the peppers and divide them equally between the cupcake liners. Pour the egg mixture on the peppers until the fill line.
5. Bake the quiches for about 20 to 25 minutes on the 'HI' setting or until set.
6. Cool the quiches in the liners for a few minutes before unmolding.
7. Repeat the process again with the remaining batter until all the quiches are done.
8. Serve hot.

13. Pecan and Maple Syrup Cinnamon Rolls

Ingredients:
- 1 - oz. (¼-stick) unsalted butter
- ¼-cup maple syrup
- ¼-cup light or medium brown sugar
- ¼-teaspoon cinnamon
- ½ (8-ounce) bag chopped pecans
- ¼-teaspoon vanilla
- 1 package raw cinnamon breakfast rolls

Instructions:
1. Place the butter, maple syrup, vanilla, brown sugar, cinnamon and pecans together in a large 10-inch baking pan. Mix well until all the ingredients are well incorporated.
2. Place the prepared baking pan on the 3-inch cooking rack and bake for 6 to 12 minutes on 350 degrees Fahrenheit.
3. Once done; add the raw cinnamon breakfast roll dough to the pan with the cinnamon side up.
4. Cover the pan with an aluminum foil and fold it over the edges firmly in order to seal it.
5. Return the pan to the oven and continue cooking for another 10 to 12 minutes at 350 degrees Fahrenheit.
6. Carefully remove the foil from the pan and continue cooking for another 10 to 12 minutes.
7. Place a serving plate upside down on the baking pan and flip it over to unmold.
8. Let the rolls cool for about 5 to 7 minutes before serving.

14. Amazingly Stuffed Banana French Toast

Ingredients:
- 1 loaf French bread (crusts removed and loaf cut into 2 1/2cm slices)
- 2 bananas; peeled and sliced diagonally
- 3 eggs; beaten
- 1/2 cup half milk; half cream
- 1 teaspoon vanilla extract
- 15ml orange liqueur
- zest of 1 orange
- 2 oz. (55g) butter

Instructions:
1. Make a cut through each slice of bread leaving the bottom intact to create a pocket and fill with 3 or 4 slices of banana in each. Pack firmly in single layer into greased pan (I use a 20cm square cake tin for this).
2. In a medium bowl beat together eggs, milk/cream, vanilla extract, orange liqueur and orange zest.
3. Pour egg mixture over bread slices in pan and allow to rest for at least 30mins. (This can be done the night before and cooked the next morning)
4. Bake in NuWave oven; 5cm rack for 25-30mins. Serve with yoghurt or crème fraiche.

15. Delicious Brekkie Muffins

Ingredients:
- 1 1/4 cup self-raising flour
- 2.3 oz. (65g) butter; melted
- 1 egg; lightly beaten
- 1/2 cup buttermilk
- 1/2 teaspoon paprika
- 2 rashers crispy bacon; chopped
- 1/2 cup grated cheese
- 1/2 cup diced tomato; seeded

Instructions:
1. Sift flour into bowl.
2. Add melted butter, egg, milk and paprika and mix well.
3. Add bacon, cheese and tomato; stir into mixture.

4. 3/4 fill silicone muffin cups or greased muffin pan and bake in NuWave oven on 2cm rack; HI for 20mins. Serve warm.

16. Quick and Easy Steak & Eggs with Cheese Stuffed Tomatoes

Ingredients:
- 2 (4-ounce) sirloin steaks
- 4 tablespoon parmesan cheese; grated
- 1 tomato; halved; seeds removed
- 2 tablespoon butter
- Seasoned salt; to taste
- 4 large eggs
- 2 scallions; thinly sliced

Instructions:
1. Slice about ¼ of the tomato from the top of each tomato half. Lightly silver the bottom of the tomato so that it can stand upright without tumbling over.
2. Place the tomato halves and the sirloin steaks on a 3-inch cooking rack.
3. Add the grated Parmesan cheese to the tomatoes.
4. Cook the steak and tomatoes on 420 degrees Fahrenheit.
5. The steak should be cooked for about 4 to 5 minutes on each side if you want a medium done steak.
6. The tomato halves need to be cooked for about 8 minutes.
7. Place a large 10.5-inch skillet on a medium flame. Add in the butter and heat for about a minute or until the butter has completely melted.
8. Add the eggs to the hot butter and cook until the whites are completely set and the yolks become firm. This should take about 3 to 4 minutes.
9. Once the steaks are done; season generously with seasoned salt.
10. Place the steaks on 2 serving plates.
11. Place the cheese stuffed tomato halves on each plates.
12. Top each steak with 2 fried eggs each.
13. Serve hot; topped with some sliced scallions.

17. Delicious Pizza with Tomato sauce

Ingredients:
- Lge rounds of pita bread
- Tomato sauce (use your own recipe or the bottled variety for spaghetti is easily found at your supermarket)
- 1 cup of pizza cheese (this is a mixture of mozzarella, parmesan; cheddar)
- Choice of toppings

Instructions:
1. Bake pita bread in NuWave oven on 10cm rack for 3mins.
2. Remove from oven and turn bread over – lightly spread this side with tomato sauce.
3. Add your choice of toppings; sprinkle with cheese.
4. Bake in NuWave oven on 10cm rack for 8mins

Note:

Suggested Toppings:
Mushrooms, capsicum, spanish onion, pineapple, olives, capers, anchovies Fresh tomato, fresh basil Prawns

18. Spinach Havarti Frittata

Ingredients:
Frittata Ingredients:
- 4 whole eggs
- 4 cups grated Havarti
- 1 cup whole milk
- 4 tablespoon extra virgin olive oil
- 2 cloves garlic; minced
- 4 cups fresh baby spinach
- Pepper; to taste
- Salt; to taste

Oven-Dried Tomatoes Ingredients:
- 12 plum tomatoes; cut in half
- 1/8 cup Kosher salt
- 1/8 cup sugar
- 1 tablespoon Herb de Provence

Instructions:
Instructions for Frittata:
1. Heat a large 10.5-inch frying pan over a medium high flame. Add in the olive oil and heat.
2. Add in the baby spinach and generously sprinkle salt and pepper to taste.
3. Cook for about 3 to 4 minutes or until the spinach wilts around the edges.
4. Transfer the spinach into a bowl and refrigerate immediately for rapid cooling.
5. In another mixing bowl; combine together eggs, cheese, garlic, milk and spinach together. Whisk well until well combined.
6. Add in salt and pepper to taste.
7. Pour the prepared frittata mixture into the liner pan and bake for about 35 to 40 minutes at 375 degrees Fahrenheit.
8. Once done; prick the center of the frittata with a toothpick. If the toothpick comes out clean the frittata is done; if not, continue cooking.

Instructions for Oven Dried Tomatoes:
1. Remove the seeds from all the plum tomato halves.
2. In a small mixing bowl; combine together the sugar, Herb de Provence and salt together. Mix lightly until well combined.
3. Sprinkle the prepared mix over the plum tomato halves, ensuring that each tomato gets a generous helping of the seasoning mix.
4. Arrange the seasoned plum tomato halves in a single layer in dehydration trays with their pulp side up.
5. Set the temperature of the dehydrator to 120 degrees and cook for a good 7 to 8 hours.

To Serve:
1. Divide the frittata into 4 equal parts.
2. Place each quarter on a serving plate.
3. Serve hot, topped with the dehydrated herbed tomatoes.

19. Corn and Bacon Pizza

Ingredients:
- 1 large round pita bread
- 1 tablespoon corn relish
- 1 rasher rindless bacon; finely chopped
- 1/4 cup grated pizza cheese (a mixture of mozzarella, parmesan & tasty cheese)
- 1 tablespoon fresh flat-leaf parsley; coarsely chopped

Instructions:
1. Spread pita bread with relish. Top with bacon and cheese.
2. Cook in NuWave Oven; on 10cm rack, for 10mins.
3. Sprinkle with parsley just before serving.

20. Egg with Manchego

Ingredients:
- 2 slices of bread
- 2 eggs
- 2 teaspoon butter or cooking spray
- 6 tablespoon Manchego cheese

Instructions:
1. Use a small round cookie cutter to remove a circle of bread from the slice.
2. Use your fingers to flatten the bread slice.
3. Apply a thin layer of butter on both sides of the bread.
4. Place the bread slices in the bottom of an oven safe baking dish.
5. Place the baking dish on a 3-inch cooking rack.
6. Carefully crack an egg into the hole in the bread slice; making sure that the egg doesn't spill out.
7. Sprinkle some black pepper on the egg and cover with a layer of Manchego cheese.
8. Repeat with the remaining bread slice.
9. Bake at 375 degrees Fahrenheit for about 7 to 10 minutes or until the egg is done to your preference.
10. Serve hot with a side of fresh fruit and some crispy bacon.

21. Amazing Breakfast Bikkies

Ingredients:
- 1 large ripe banana (the riper the better)
- 3/4 cup granulated sugar
- 3/4 cup peanut butter
- 1/4 cup water
- 2 egg whites
- 1 cup plain flour
- 1/2 cup whole wheat plain flour
- 1/2 teaspoon baking soda
- 1/2 teaspoon salt
- 2 cups quick-cooking rolled oats
- 1/2 cups chopped walnuts
- 1/4 cup chocolate chips

Instructions:

1. In a large mixing bowl; mash banana. With electric mixer, beat in sugar, peanut butter, water and egg whites until smooth.
2. Add sifted flours, baking soda and salt.
3. Stir in remaining ingredients. Take tablespoonfuls of mixture and roll into a ball. Flatten balls with palms of hands and place on 5cm rack.
4. Bake in NuWave oven for 15mins; turn over and bake a further 2mins.
5. Allow to cool on wire rack.

22. Tasty Baked Eggs with Cherry Tomatoes and Spinach

Ingredients:
- 8 eggs
- 2/3 Cup (150g) baby spinach leaves
- 12 cherry tomatoes cut into halves
- 3.5 oz. (100g) Gruyere cheese; grated
- Cayenne pepper & salt

Instructions:
1. Blanch spinach in boiling salted water until just wilted. Drain well and squeeze out excess water.
2. Divide spinach into 4 x 1-cup greased ramekins.
3. Break 2 eggs into each ramekin and top each one with 6 cherry tomatoes halves.
4. Sprinkle with cayenne pepper and salt and top with grated cheese.
5. Bake in NuWave oven; on 5cm rack for 15mins or until eggs are set to your liking.
6. Serve with crispy bacon, chipolatas and crunchy toast fingers.

23. Easy Crunchy French Toast

Ingredients:
- 1/4 loaf bread (any type); chopped into thick sliced
- 1/2 cup corn flakes; crumbed
- 1/2 (16-ounce) container egg substitute

Instructions:
1. Pour the egg substitute in a shallow pan.
2. Place the bread slices in the egg substitute and soak for a minute or two.
3. Place the crumbled cornflakes in a flat dish and coat the egg substitute-soaked bread slices with the crumbled cornflakes.
4. Place the bread slices on the 3-inch rack and bake on the 'HI' setting for about 12 to 15 minutes.
5. Allow to cool a bit before serving with a side of fresh fruit or a dollop of whipped cream if you wish.

24. Smoked Salmon Quesadilla with Cream Chives and Cheese

Ingredients:
- 4 (8-inch) flour tortillas
- Freshly ground black pepper; to taste
- ¼-pound good-quality smoked salmon
- 3 - oz. whipped cream cheese and chives (approximately 6 tablespoons)
- 2 teaspoon olive oil

Instructions:
1. Pace 2 flour tortillas on a flat working surface.
2. Spread each tortilla with about 3 tablespoons of the whipped cream cheese and chives. Make sure you leave about ½ inch from all the edges.
3. Slice the smoked salmon into 1-inch strips and divide into two equal halves.
4. Spread each half of the salmons onto the cream cheese covered tortillas.
5. Sprinkle some freshly ground black pepper over the salmon pieces.
6. Place the remaining tortillas over the salmon and lightly press down.
7. Spread about ½ teaspoon of the olive oil on each tortilla and flip onto the 4-inch cooking rack.
8. Brush the remaining oil over the tortillas.
9. Cook on the HI power level for about 4 to 6 minutes on each side.
10. Slice into manageable pieces and serve hot with a side of your favorite salsa.

SNACKS & APPETIZERS

25. *Delicious Cheesy Mixed Vegetable Quesadillas*

Ingredients:

- 1/2 small zucchini; grated and drained
- 1/2 small red onion; chopped
- 1/2 cup frozen corn; defrosted and drained
- 1 jalapeño pepper; seeded and chopped
- 1/4 teaspoon salt
- 1/2 (15-ounce) can black beans; drained and rinsed
- 1/8 teaspoon freshly ground black pepper
- 1/2-pound Monterey-Jack cheese; grated
- 1/2 teaspoon chili powder
- 4 (8-inch) flour tortillas
- 1 tablespoon vegetable oil

Instructions:

1. Place the zucchini, onion, beans, pepper, corn, jalapeños, salt and chili powder together in a large mixing bowl. Toss well until well-seasoned.
2. Place the tortillas in a single layer on a 3-inch rack.
3. Divide the vegetable mixture into 4 parts and place each part on a tortilla. Sprinkle each tortilla with a good amount of cheese.
4. Bake the tortillas on the 'HI' setting for about 5 to 7 minutes or until the cheese has melted.
5. Remove tortillas from the oven and fold into half.
6. Slice the quesadillas into halves and serve with your favorite salsa or with a condiment of your choice.

26. *Toasted Bacon and Grilled Cheese, Apple Sandwiches*

Ingredients:

- 4 tablespoons butter; softened
- 8 slices sourdough bread
- 12 ounces smoked Gouda cheese; sliced
- 12 strips apple wood smoked beef bacon; cooked
- 2 honey crisp apples; cored and sliced
- Salt to taste

Instructions:

1. Apply about 1/2 tablespoon of butter on one side of the sourdough bread slice.
2. With the buttered slice up; place four slices of the buttered bread on a 3-inch rack.
3. Toast the bread on the 'HI' setting for about 3 to 4 minutes.
4. Flip the bread over and place about 3 strips of beef bacon and 1 slice of cheese on each slice of the bread.
5. Place the apple slices in a single layer over the cheese.
6. Place the remaining buttered slices over the apple slices with their buttered side up.
7. Toast the sandwiches for another 4 to 5 minutes on the 'HI' setting.
8. Once toasted; remove the toasted sandwiches on a cutting board and slice diagonally before serving.
9. Serve warm.

27. Delicious Cheese Stuffed Mushroom Caps

Ingredients:
- ½ garlic clove; finely chopped
- 2 tablespoon olive oil; divided
- ¼-cup finely chopped roasted red pepper
- ½ teaspoon finely chopped fresh sage
- 2 - oz. shredded mozzarella cheese
- Pinch salt
- 12 small mushroom caps; stems removed

Instructions:
1. Combine together garlic, 1-tablespoon olive oil, salt, red pepper and sage together in a medium sized mixing bowl. Mix well until well combined.
2. Add in the shredded mozzarella cheese and keep mixing.
3. In another bowl; place the mushroom caps. Pour the remaining olive oil over them and toss well until well coated.
4. Spoon the prepared cheese mixture into the oil coated mushroom caps.
5. Place the stuffed mushroom caps in a single layer on the 3-inch cooking rack.
6. Bake for about 5 to 7 minutes at 350 degrees Fahrenheit.
7. When done; remove the mushrooms from the oven and cool until handle able.
8. Serve warm with a condiment of your choice.

28. Sour Cream and Ranch Stuff Potato Bites

Ingredients:
- 4 medium baked potatoes
- 2 packets ranch seasoning
- 1/2 cup low fat sour cream
- 2 cups Cheddar cheese; shredded
- Beef Bacon pieces; cooked (optional)
- Green onions (optional)

Instructions:
1. Place the potatoes on the 1-inch rack and lightly fork. Bake them on the 'HI' setting for about 45 to 50 minutes.
2. Remove the potatoes from the oven and cool for about 5 to 10 minutes.
3. Cut the potatoes in halves, lengthwise and use a spoon to scoop out the filling from the skin.
4. Place the potato in a mixing bowl. Add in the seasoning mix and the low fat sour cream to it. Mix well until well combined.
5. Spoon the prepared mixture into the skins and top with some cheese.
6. Place the prepared skins on a 3-inch rack and bake on the 'HI' setting for about 7 to 10 minutes or until the cheese is bubbly.
7. Top with beef bacon and green onions and serve immediately.

29. Goat Cheese and Walnut, Pear Crostini

Ingredients:
- 1/4 cup coarsely chopped walnuts
- 1/2 tablespoon brown sugar

- 1/2 tablespoon plus 1 teaspoon honey
- 1 large Bosc pear; peeled, cored and cut lengthwise into wedges about 1/2-inch thick
- 1 (6-inch) baguette
- 1/2 tablespoon olive oil
- 3 ounces' goat cheese
- Extra-virgin olive oil
- 1/2 cup arugula or basil (optional)
- Coarse sea salt or kosher salt

Instructions:
1. Place the walnuts in a small mixing bowl. Add in the 1-teaspoon honey and the brown sugar. Toss well until the walnuts are well coated.
2. Place the walnuts in a single layer in the liner pan. Place the 3-inch rack over the walnut filled liner pan.
3. Slice the baguette into 1/2-inch thick slices and arrange on the 3-inch rack in a single layer.
4. Lightly brush olive oil over the baguette slices.
5. Set your NuWave oven on the 'HI' setting and toast the bread and walnuts for about 4 to 5 minutes.
6. Remove the bread covered 3-inch rack from the oven and toast the walnuts for an additional 4 to 6 minutes.
7. Place the toasted bread slices on a flat surface and arrange the pear wedges on the bread in a single layer.
8. Spread the goat cheese on the pears.
9. Top the cheese with the toasted walnuts and garnish with some basil or arugula.
10. Lightly pour some olive oil and honey over the crostini and season to taste with a pinch of kosher salt or sea salt.
11. Rest the crostini for about 30 minutes before serving. This helps in enhancing the cheesy flavor in the crostini.
12. Serve with a side of toasted walnuts.

30. Tasty Garlic Buttermilk Biscuit Bread Bites

Ingredients:
- 1/2 (16-ounce) tube refrigerated buttermilk biscuits
- 1 tablespoon freshly grated Parmesan
- 2 tablespoons unsalted butter; melted
- 2 cloves garlic; minced
- 1/4 teaspoon dried basil
- 1/4 teaspoon dried oregano
- 1/4 teaspoon dried parsley flakes
- Pinch of salt

Instructions:
1. Arrange 6 silicon cupcake liners on the 1-inch rack.
2. Place the refrigerated buttermilk biscuit dough on a flat and floured work surface
3. Using an extremely sharp knife cut every piece of the buttermilk biscuit dough into 8 even slices. Keep aside.
4. Place the butter, garlic, basil, salt, Parmesan, oregano and parsley together in a large mixing bowl. Whisk together using a wire whisk until its gets a smooth texture.

5. Pour about 1 tablespoon of the prepared herb butter mixture into a small bowl and keep aside.
6. Place the biscuit pieces into the herbed butter mix and toss until well coated.
7. Take about 5 to 7 slices of the herbed butter covered dough and press them together in the bottom of each greased cupcake liner.
8. Add the extender ring to the base tray of your NuWave oven.
9. Close the dome of your NuWave oven and bake on the '8' setting of your NuWave oven for about 18 to 20 minutes.
10. Using a pastry brush, lightly brush the reserved herbed butter mix onto the bread bites and serve immediately.

Tips:
1. If you do not wish to bake individual muffin cups, bake the bread bites in a loaf pan or a divided silicon baking pan on the 1-inch rack on the '8' setting for 28 to 30 minutes.
2. You can use any other cheese, such as mozzarella or Cheddar or even Gouda cheese instead of Parmesan cheese.

31. Tasty Herb Cheese Fries

Ingredients:
- 1/2 pound 3-cheese blend; shredded
- 1/2 tablespoon fresh thyme; chopped
- 1/2 tablespoon fresh oregano; chopped
- 1/2 tablespoon fresh rosemary; chopped
- 1/4 teaspoon freshly ground black pepper
- 1-pound frozen fries
- Pinch of kosher salt
- 1 tablespoon olive oil

Instructions:
1. Place the fresh thyme, fresh rosemary, fresh oregano, freshly ground black pepper and kosher salt together in a small mixing bowl. Mix well until well combined.
2. Place the frozen fries in a large mixing bowl and pour the olive oil over the frozen fries. Toss well until the fries are well coated with olive oil.
3. Pour the seasoning mix over the olive oil coated fries and toss well until the fries are well coated with the seasoning.
4. Place the seasoning coated fries on the 3-inch rack in an even layer.
5. Set your NuWave oven on the 'HI' setting and bake for about 8 to 10 minutes.
6. Once the fries get a crispy exterior; open the dome of your NuWave oven and transfer the fries from the 3-inch rack to the liner pan.
7. Top the fries with the shredded 3 cheese blend and bake for another 5 to 7 minutes on the 'HI' setting or until the cheese has melted.
8. Once the fries are done; promptly open the dome of the oven so that all the excess moisture is released and the fries remain crispy.
9. Serve hot.

Tips:
1. If you do not have fresh spices; you can use the dried ones too. Just halve the quantity of spices.
2. When the fries are baking initially; make sure you pause the oven at regular intervals to toss the fries. This ensures that all the fries are evenly browned.
3. If you are using fresh potatoes instead of the frozen fries, add about 5 minutes to the total cooking time.

32. Caramel Glaze Chicken Skewers

Ingredients:
- 1 tablespoon fish sauce
- ½ tablespoon orange juice
- ½ tablespoon light brown sugar
- 1 3/4 pounds skinless chicken breasts; cut into 1-inch chunks
- 1/8 cup white sesame seeds
- 6-inch bamboo skewers
- 1/6 cup sliced almonds
- 1/8 cup black sesame seeds

Ingredients for the Caramel Glaze:
- 1/6 cup fish sauce
- 1/3 cup light brown sugar
- 1/6 cup orange juice
- 1/6 cup rice wine vinegar
- 1 tablespoon honey
- ½ tablespoon garlic; minced
- ½ (1-inch) piece fresh ginger; minced
- 1 shallot; chopped

Instructions:
1. In a small mixing bowl; whisk together the fish sauce, orange juice and brown sugar using a wire whisk. Whisk well until all the ingredients are incorporated.
2. Soak the bamboo skewers in some warm water for 6 to 8 hours.
3. Thread the chicken pieces on to the bamboo skewers.
4. Place the skewers in a large bowl and pour the prepared marinade over them. Toss well to coat.
5. Cover the bow and refrigerate for about 3 to 4 hours.
6. In another bowl; combine together the remaining fish sauce, brown sugar, orange juice, rice wine vinegar, honey, garlic, ginger and shallot together. Whisk well until well combined.
7. Combine the almonds and sesame seeds and spread in an even layer in the bottom of a pizza liner pan. If you do not have a pizza liner pan, just use a small cookie sheet.
8. Place the pizza liner pan on the 3-inch cooking rack and toast for about 3 to 5 minutes on 350 degrees Fahrenheit. Keep aside.
9. Place the marinated chicken skewers on the 3-inch cooking rack and lightly brush the prepared caramel glaze over them.
10. Bake for about 7 to 10 minutes at 350 degrees Fahrenheit.
11. Flip the chicken skewers over and brush some caramel glaze over them. Continue baking for another 7 to 10 minutes.

12. Place the prepared chicken skewers on a serving platter and serve hot topped with the prepared toasted almonds and sesame seeds.

33. Toasted Pita Chips with Garlic and Artichoke Dip

Ingredients:
- ½ (12-ounce) can medium diced artichokes; drained
- 2 cups Monterey Jack cheese; shredded and divided
- 1 tablespoon fresh garlic; minced
- ½-cup heavy cream
- 1/8 cup parmesan cheese
- ¼-cup mayonnaise
- ¼-cup bread crumbs
- White pepper; to taste
- Salt; to taste
- ½ package of fresh pita chips
- 1/8 cup parmesan cheese
- 1/8 cup olive oil
- ¼-cup finely chopped parsley

Instructions:
1. Combine the diced artichokes, 1-cup Monterey Jack cheese, cream, breadcrumbs, pepper, garlic, mayonnaise, Parmesan cheese and salt together in a large mixing bowl. Mix well until all the ingredients are well combined.
2. Pour this mix into a large 10-inch baking pan and even the top out using the back of a spoon or a spatula.
3. Top with the remaining Monterey Jack cheese.
4. Place the baking dish on the 1-inch cooking rack and bake on the HI power setting for about 10 to 12 minutes or until the filling is hot and the top has browned.
5. While the dip cooks, cut the pita bread into about 6 pieces per slice.
6. Place the pita chips in a bowl and pour the olive oil over them. Toss well to coat.
7. Place the chips on the 4-inch cooking rack in a single layer and toast for about 3 to 4 minutes on the HI power setting or until evenly browned.
8. Place the toasted pita chips in a bowl and top with parsley, pepper, Parmesan cheese and salt. Toss well to coat.
9. Serve immediately with the prepared dip on the side.

34. Fried Ravioli

Ingredients:
- ¼-cup all-purpose flour
- Pepper; to taste
- Salt; to taste
- 2 eggs
- ¼-cup breadcrumbs
- 5 ravioli; frozen
- 1 tablespoon chopped parsley
- 1 tablespoon parmesan cheese

Optional Ingredients:
- Basil
- Marinara sauce

Instructions:
1. Sieve together the salt, flour and pepper together in a small mixing bowl. Keep aside.

2. In another small mixing bowl; crack open the eggs and whisk well until lightly frothy.
3. In a third small mixing bowl; add in the basil and breadcrumbs and mix well until well combined.
4. Place the ravioli in the flour mix and toss well until well coated.
5. Dunk the flour covered ravioli into the whisked egg and shake of the excess.
6. Finally; roll the egg-covered ravioli in the breadcrumb mixture.
7. Repeat with the remaining ravioli.
8. Place the breaded ravioli in a single layer on the 3-inch cooking rack.
9. Cook for about 8 to 10 minutes at 400 degrees Fahrenheit.
10. Once the ravioli is cooked through, top with parsley and Parmesan.
11. Serve hot with some marinara sauce.

35. Delicious Triple Cheese Garlic Bread

Ingredients:
- 1/2 loaf Italian bread; sliced in half
- 1 cloves minced garlic
- 3 tablespoons olive oil
- 1/4 teaspoon dried oregano
- 1/2 cup shredded Asiago cheese
- 1 tablespoons grated Parmesan cheese
- 1/2 cup mozzarella cheese

Instructions:
1. Combine the garlic, olive oil and oregano together in a small mixing bowl.
2. Using a pastry brush, brush the prepared mix onto the cut sides of the bread.
3. In a medium sized mixing bowl; place the Asiago cheese and top with the Parmesan cheese. Add in the mozzarella cheese and mix well until combined.
4. Place the garlic and olive oil brushed bread with its cut side up on the 1-inch rack.
5. Top the bread with a copious amount of cheese and bake on the 'HI' setting for about 12 to 15 minutes or until the cheese has completely melted.
6. Cool the bread a little, and once slightly firm, slice the bread into 1/2-inch slices.
7. Serve immediately; topped with some chili flakes and pizza seasoning.

36. Spicy and Sweet Roasted Nuts

Ingredients:
- 1 ½ tablespoon sugar
- ½ teaspoon paprika
- ¼-teaspoon salt
- ½ teaspoon ground cinnamon
- Pinch ground cloves
- ¼-teaspoon ground cumin
- ½ large egg white
- 1 cup pecans
- 1 cup walnuts

Instructions:
1. Combine together the sugar, paprika, salt, ground cinnamon, ground cloves and ground cumin together in a small mixing bowl. Keep aside.
2. Whisk the egg white until lightly frothy.

3. Add the pecans and walnuts to the whisked egg white and mix well.
4. Pour the prepared spice mix onto the egg white coated nuts and toss well until well coated.
5. Spread the prepared nut mix in the bottom of the liner pan and cook for about 25 minutes at 350 degrees Fahrenheit.
6. Pause the oven around the 12-minute mark and mix well.
7. Rest in the oven until the pan is cool enough to handle.
8. Cool the nuts completely before serving.
9. Store the leftover nuts (if any) in an airtight jar, at room temperature, away from direct sunlight. The shelf life of these nuts is 3 days.

37. Amazing Bacon Wrapped Shrimp Bites

Ingredients:
- 6 jumbo shrimp; cut in half or 12 small shrimp
- 3 slices beef bacon
- 1/8 cup sliced water chestnuts

Instructions:
1. Chop the beef bacon into 4 equal parts.
2. Place a chestnut slice on a shrimp.
3. Roll the bacon carefully over the shrimp and chestnut and secure it in place using a toothpick.
4. Place the prepared shrimp rolls on the 3-inch rack and bake on the 'HI' setting for about 8 to 10 minutes per side.
5. Serve hot with a side of your favorite condiment and a fresh salad.

Note:
You can also use tofu, mussels or chicken livers in place of the shrimp.

38. Tasty Corn and Jalapeño Cheddar, Muffins

Ingredients:
- 1/2 cup Cheddar cheese; shredded
- 3/4 cups flour
- 1/2 cup sugar
- 3/4 cups cornmeal
- 1/2 teaspoon baking powder
- 1/2 teaspoon salt
- 1/4 teaspoon baking soda
- 5 tablespoons milk
- 5 tablespoons sour cream
- 1/2 stick butter
- 1/2 jalapeño; chopped and seeded
- 1 egg
- 1/2 onion; diced and caramelized

Instructions:
1. Combine the flour, sugar, cornmeal, baking powder, salt and baking soda together in a medium sized mixing bowl.
2. In another bowl; combine Cheddar cheese, milk, sour cream, butter jalapeños, egg and onion together.
3. Pour the wet ingredients onto the dry ingredients and fold well until well combined. Do not over mix or the batter will fall flat.

4. Spray 6 muffin cups with cooking spray or grease them using a little melted butter.
5. Pour the batter into the 6 prepared muffin cups.
6. Place the batter filed cups on the 3-inch rack and bake on the 'HI' setting for about 20 to 25 minutes.
7. Remove the muffin cups from the oven and cool for about 5 minutes.
8. Remove the muffins from the muffin cups and cool on a wire rack for about 10 to 15 minutes.
9. Serve warm with a side of your favorite salsa or condiment.

39. Tasty NuWave Nachos

Ingredients:
- 1/2 bag tortilla chips
- 1/2 package taco seasoning
- 1/2-pound cooked ground beef
- 2 tomatoes; diced
- 1/2 jar pickled jalapeños
- 1/2 can sliced olives
- 1/2 jar salsa
- 1/2 bag shredded Cheddar cheese
- 1/4 cup sour cream

Instructions:
1. Pour the tortilla chips into the liner pan and arrange in an even layer.
2. Place the ground beef in a mixing bowl and sprinkle the taco seasoning over it. Mix well until combined.
3. Spread the ground beef over the tacos in an even layer.
4. Top the beef with the tomatoes, salsa, jalapeños and sour cream.
5. Pour the cheese generously over the veggies and bake on the 'HI' setting for about 10 to 15 minutes or until the cheese is bubbling.
6. Remove the nachos from the oven and cool.
7. Serve immediately.

40. Corn, Zucchini and Black Bean Quesadillas

Ingredients:
- ½ small zucchini; grated and drained
- ½ small red onion; chopped
- ½-cup frozen corn; defrosted and drained
- 1 jalapeno pepper; seeded and chopped
- ¼-teaspoon salt
- ½ (15-ounce) can black beans; drained and rinsed
- 1/8 teaspoon freshly ground black pepper
- ½ pound Monterey Jack cheese; grated
- ½ teaspoon chili powder
- 1 tablespoon vegetable oil
- 4 (8-inch) flour tortillas

Instructions:
1. Place the zucchini, onion, beans, pepper, corn, jalapenos, salt and chili powder together in a large mixing bowl. Toss well until all the ingredients are well coated with the seasoning.
2. Add in the cheese and mix well.

3. Place the tortillas on a floured flat work surface.
4. Scoop about ¼ of the prepared vegetable filling onto one half of a tortilla. Spread into and even layer using the back of a spoon, ensuring that the filling doesn't touch the edge of the tortilla.
5. Fold the tortillas in half over the filling.
6. Place the prepared quesadillas on the 3-inch cooking rack and cook for about 4 to 5 minutes per side at 350 degrees Fahrenheit.
7. Cut the quesadillas into halves and serve warm with your favorite condiment.

41. Garlic Bread

Ingredients:
- ½ loaf Italian bread sliced in half
- 1 clove garlic; minced
- 3 tablespoon olive oil
- ¼-teaspoon dried oregano
- ½-cup shredded Asiago
- 1 tablespoon grated Parmesan cheese
- ½-cup Mozzarella cheese

Instructions:
1. Combine the olive oil, oregano and garlic together in a small bow. Whisk well until well combined.
2. Use a pastry brush to brush the cut sides of the bread with prepared herbed olive oil on it.
3. In another mixing bowl combine the Asiago cheese, Parmesan cheese and Mozzarella cheese together.
4. Divide the cheese equally amongst the bread slices, sprinkling generously on the cut sides.
5. Place the cheese covered bread on the 1-inch cooking rack and bake on the HI power setting for about 12 to 14 minutes or until the cheese is melted and bubbly.
6. Slice the garlic bread and serve immediately topped with some red chili flakes.

42. Succulent Italian Bread Loaf Pizza

Ingredients:
- 2 (12-inch) loaves Italian bread
- 4 tablespoons olive oil
- 2 tablespoon garlic; chopped
- 1 cup marinara sauce
- 2/3 cup Parmesan cheese; shredded
- 6 baby Portabella mushrooms; sliced
- 2/3 cup red onions; sliced
- 2/3 cup green pepper; sliced
- 1/2 cup tomato; diced
- 1 cup mozzarella cheese; shredded
- 2 tablespoons basil; sliced

Instructions:
1. Slice the loaves of bread in half lengthwise. Use a serrated knife dipped into hot water (and wiped before cutting) for best results.
2. Combine the olive oil and chopped garlic together in a small bowl and set aside for about 5 to 10 minutes so that the olive oil gets infused with the garlic.
3. Using a pastry brush spread the prepared garlic olive oil on the bread.

4. Using a spoon spread the marinara sauce in a thin layer over the bread. Top the marinara sauce layer with an even layer of Parmesan cheese.
5. Add the mushrooms, peppers, onions and tomatoes over the Parmesan cheese and top the vegetables with a layer of mozzarella cheese.
6. Place the prepared bread loaf halves on a 1-inch rack and bake on the 'HI' setting for about 10 minutes or until the cheese melts.
7. Garnish the pizza with some basil.
8. Slice your pizza and serve immediately.

43. Yummy Cheesy Bacon and Tater Tot Bombs

Ingredients:
- 1 cup frozen tater tots; brought to room temperature
- 2 slices bacon; quartered
- ½ - oz. sharp cheddar cheese; cut into ¼-inch squares
- 1/8 cup brown sugar

Optional Ingredients:
- ½ tablespoon chopped parsley

Instructions:
1. Place a tater tot on a cheese square.
2. Holding them into place; wrap a single bacon slice around both tightly.
3. Place the brown sugar in a flat plate.
4. Roll the bacon covered tater tot and cheese squares in the brown sugar, pressing lightly, until covered in a layer of brown sugar.
5. Carefully arrange the tater tots in the liner pan in a single layer, with their seam side down.
6. Bake for about 25 to 30 minutes at 350 degrees Fahrenheit.
7. Around the 12-minute mark; flip the tater tot over to ensure even browning.
8. Top with some parsley and serve hot.

44. Amazing Beefy Bacon Wrapped Tater Tots

Ingredients:
- 1 cup frozen tater tots; brought down to room temperature
- 1/2-ounce sharp Cheddar cheese; cut into 1/4-inch squares
- 2 slices beef bacon; cut into quarters
- 2 tablespoons brown sugar
- 1/2 tablespoon chopped parsley (optional)

Instructions:
1. Wrap a piece of beef bacon around a tater tot and cheese square.
2. Place the brown sugar in a flat plate and lightly roll the beef bacon wrapped tater tots in the brown sugar. Lightly press while rolling to ensure that the brown sugar sticks to the surface of the beef bacon.
3. Place the beef bacon wrapped and brown sugar covered tater tots on the liner pan, with their seam side facing down.

4. Bake on the 'HI' setting for about 25 to 30 minutes. Make sure you flip the tater tots over around the halfway mark.
5. Serve immediately; topped with some parsley.

45. Delicious Cereal Party Mix

Ingredients:
- 1 cup bite size corn square cereal
- 1/2 cup pretzel knots
- 1 cup bite size rice square cereal
- 1/8 cup packed brown sugar
- 1/4 cup sliced almonds
- 3/4 tablespoon butter
- 1/8 teaspoon baking soda
- 3/4 tablespoon light-colored corn syrup
- 1/4 cup dried cranberries

Instructions:
1. Place the bite size corn cereal, bite size rice cereal, almond and pretzels together in a large bowl. Mix well and keep aside.
2. Place the brown sugar, corn syrup and butter together in a large saucepan.
3. Heat on a medium high flame and keep mixing until the mixtures starts bubbling lightly.
4. Stop stirring and let the mixture simmer for another 3 to 4 minutes.
5. Take the saucepan off heat and add in the baking soda. Mix well.
6. Pour the prepared sugar mixture over the prepared cereal mix and toss well until well coated.
7. Pour the prepared cereal and sugar mix on the liner pan in a single layer.
8. Bake on the 'HI' setting for about 9 to 10 minutes.
9. Remove the pan from the oven and stir well using a wooden spoon.
10. Pop the liner pan back into the NuWave oven and bake for another 5 to 7 minutes.
11. Lightly grease a sheet of aluminum foil with some butter or spray with cooking spray and empty the hot party mix onto it.
12. Once cooled; break the party mix into pieces and add in the dried fruit.
13. Mix well and serve immediately.
14. Store in an airtight container, away from direct sunlight.

46. Cheesy Nachos

Ingredients:
- ½ bag tortilla chips
- ½ pound cooked ground beef
- ½ package taco seasoning
- 2 tomatoes; diced
- ½ can sliced olives
- ½ jar pickled jalapenos
- ½ jar salsa
- ¼-cup sour cream
- ½ bag shredded cheddar cheese

Instructions:
1. Pour the tortilla chips directly into the liner pan.
2. Combine the ground beef with the taco seasoning and then spread over the taco chips in an even layer.

3. In a small mixing bowl combine together the tomatoes, jalapenos, sour cream, olives and salsa.
4. Mix well and pour over the ground beef.
5. Alternatively; you can layer each individual ingredient beginning with tomato, followed by olives and jalapenos, topped with a layer of salsa topped with a layer of sour cream.
6. Pour the cheese over the nachos and pop the liner pan into your NuWave Oven.
7. Bake at 350 degrees Fahrenheit for about 10 to 15 minutes.
8. Let the nachos cool before serving.

47. Apple Jelly Glazed Chicken Wings

Ingredients:
- 1 tablespoon all-purpose flour
- ¼-teaspoon dried garlic
- ½ teaspoon salt
- ¼-teaspoon dried onion
- 1-pound chicken wings
- ½ teaspoon smoked paprika
- 1 ¼-tablespoon cayenne pepper sauce
- 1 tablespoon apple jelly; melted
- 1 tablespoon unsalted butter; melted
- Chipotle peppers in adobo sauce

Instructions:
1. Combine the flour, garlic, paprika, salt and onion together in a large mixing bowl.
2. Add the chicken to the flour mix and toss well until well coated.
3. Place the flour coated chicken thighs on the 3-inch cooking rack.
4. Pop the rack into the oven and bake the chicken for about 40 to 45 minutes at 350 degrees Fahrenheit. Flip the chicken over around the 20-minute mark for even browning.
5. While the chicken roasts in the oven; place the hot sauce, butter, apple jelly and chipotle peppers together in a small mixing bowl. Whisk well until combined.
6. Place the roasted chicken wings on a serving platter and drizzle the prepared sauce over them.
7. Serve hot with a side of pan-fried veggies.

48. Orleans Style Crab Cakes

Ingredients:
- 1 tablespoon Dijon mustard
- ½-cup beef broth
- ¼-cup grain mustard
- 1/8 cup white wine
- 8 - oz. pasteurized crab meat (lump or claw meat)
- ½-cup heavy cream
- ½ tablespoon chives; finely diced
- 1/3 cup celery; finely diced
- 1 tablespoon red pepper; finely diced
- 1 ½ ounces; Japanese Panko breadcrumbs
- Salt; to taste
- ½ egg
- Old Bay Seasoning; to taste
- Pepper; to taste

Instructions:
1. Heat a 3.5 to 4-quart pot over a medium flame. Add in the grain mustard, white wine, Dijon mustard and beef broth to it. Continue heating until the liquid is lightly bubbling.
2. Pour in the cream and mix well until well blended.
3. Lower the heat to a medium low and heat for another 10 minutes or until the sauce is thick enough to coat the back of a spoon.
4. Take the sauce off the heat and keep aside, but ensure it remains warm.
5. In a mixing bowl; combine together the crabmeat, red pepper, Panko, salt, Old Bay seasoning, chives, celery, egg, and pepper together. Fold well until all the ingredients are well combined.
6. Divide the mix into three equal parts and make crab patties that are 1-inch thick and 3-inches wide from each third.
7. Tear sheet of foil large enough to cover your cooking rack. Cover the 1-inch cooking rack with the foil and grease the foil with some butter or spray some cooking spray over it.
8. Place the prepared 3 crab cakes on the greased foil.
9. Bake on the HI power setting for 5 to 7 minutes, flipping it over around the 3-minute mark.
10. Serve hot with some mustard sauce on the side.

49. Jalapeno and Cheddar Muffins

Ingredients:
- 3/4 cup flour
- ½-cup sugar
- 3/4 cup cornmeal
- ½ teaspoon baking powder
- ½ teaspoon salt
- ¼-teaspoon baking soda
- 1/3 cup sour cream
- ½ stick butter
- 1/3 cup milk
- 1 egg
- ½ onion; diced and caramelized
- ½ jalapeno; chopped and seeded
- ½-cup cheddar cheese; shredded

Instructions:
1. Combine the flour, sugar, cornmeal, baking powder, salt and baking soda together in a large mixing bowl. Mix well until all the ingredients are well incorporated.
2. In another mixing bowl; pour in the sour cream, butter, milk and egg together. Whisk until all the ingredients are well emulsified.
3. Slowly add the flour mix into the sour cream mix, making sure that there are no lumps.
4. Add the caramelized onions, jalapenos and cheddar cheese to the batter and mix well.
5. Grease 6 muffin cups with some butter or spray them with some cooking spray.
6. Divide the batter among the 6 muffin cups.
7. Place the cups on the 3-inch cooking rack.
8. Bake the muffins at 350 degrees Fahrenheit for about 15 to 20 minutes or until a knife run through the center of the muffin comes out clean.
9. Cool the muffins on a wire rack before serving.

50. Chicken, Asparagus and Corn Tarts

Ingredients:
- 3 sheets frozen ready-rolled puff pastry; partially thawed
- 2 teaspoon olive oil
- 7 oz. (200g) chicken mince
- 2 green onions; thinly sliced
- 3 eggs
- 1/2 cup pure cream
- 1/2 x 11 oz. (340g) bottle asparagus; drained, trimmed, cut into 1cm pieces
- 4.5 oz. (125g) can corn kernels; drained
- 1/3 cup grated tasty cheese

Instructions:
1. Cut each pasty sheet into 4 square. Using 2 x 6-cup greased muffin pans, press 1 square into each pan hole.
2. Heat oil in a frying pan over medium-high heat. Add mince and onion; cook, stirring with a wooden spoon to break up mince, for 3-4 minutes or until mince is browned.
3. Whisk eggs and cream together in a jug. Season with pepper and salt.
4. Divide mince mixture between pan holes. Top with asparagus, corn and egg mixture. Sprinkle with cheese.
5. Bake in NuWave oven on 5cm rack; power level HI, for 20 mins; Carefully remove tarts from pan and place directly onto the 5cm rack and bake for a further 5 mins.

51. Nuwave Style Pesto Stars

Ingredients:
- 1 oz. (30g) butter; softened
- 2 sheets puff pastry; thawed
- 2 tablespoon pesto (this can be basil; sun dried tomato or your favorite)
- 1/2 cup parmesan cheese; finely grated

Instructions:
1. Combine pesto and butter in a small bowl.
2. Spread pesto mixture over pastry sheets, sprinkle with cheese.
3. Using a star shaped pastry cutter; cut stars from pasty sheets, place onto baking paper or well oiled 10cm rack.
4. Bake in NuWave oven on 10cm rack; level 10 for 5mins; turning for last minute if you wish.

52. Nuwave Style Hommus

Ingredients:
- 7 oz. (200g) chick peas; drained
- 1/4 cup vegetable stock
- 2 cloves garlic
- 2 tablespoon lemon juice
- 2 tablespoon tahini

Instructions:
1. Place everything in the tall cup fitted with the cross-blade.
2. Blend until smooth.

53. Tasty Crunchy Sausage Rolls

Ingredients:
- 1 sheet puff pastry
- 8.8 oz. (250g) beef mince
- 1 stick celery; very finely chopped
- 1/2 teaspoon Worcestershire sauce
- 1 teaspoon tomato sauce
- 1 teaspoon corn flour
- 1 egg; lightly beaten (for egg wash)

Instructions:
1. Mix mince, celery, sauces and corn flour together.
2. Cut pastry into 16 squares (4 down and 4 across).
3. Shape teaspoons of meat mixture into balls and roll into 5cm sausages. Place diagonally onto pastry square and pinch other corners together.
4. Brush each sausage roll with egg wash. Cover 10cm rack with a piece of baking paper and place rolls onto paper.
5. Bake in NuWave oven (level 10); 10cm rack, for 15 minutes, turning over for last 5 minutes.

54. Vegetable and Chicken Pies

Ingredients:
- 1 tablespoon olive oil
- 1 oz. (30g) butter
- 18 oz. (500g) chicken breast filler; cut into 2cm chunks
- 1 leek; white part only; finely sliced
- 1 garlic clove; crushed
- 1 tablespoon flour
- 1/3 cup water
- 1 cup chicken stock
- 1/2 cup thick cream
- 1 large carrot; peeled; cooked, diced
- 1 large potato; peeled, boiled, diced
- 1 cup frozen peas; cooked
- 1 tablespoon chopped fresh or 1/2 teaspoon dried tarragon
- 4 sheets puff pastry; thawed
- 1 egg; lightly beaten

Instructions:
1. Heat olive oil and butter in a frypan over medium heat, add pieces of chicken and cook until lightly browned and almost cooked through. Transfer chicken to a plate and set aside.
2. Add leek and garlic to the pan and cook over low heat for 2-3 minutes or until softened.
3. Add the flour and cook for 1min. Add water and bring to the boil for 1min; then pour in stock and cream and cook; stirring, for a further 5 minutes over medium-low heat.
4. Return chicken to pan with cooked vegetables and tarragon, season well, then set aside to cool.
5. Cut each pastry square into 4 squares. Place some chicken mixture in the centre of each square, then lift up the sides of the pastry to form a parcel, pinching edges together to seal. Twist top join around decoratively.
6. Place on small rounds of baking paper and brush pies with beaten egg. Bake in NuWave oven on 10cm rack; level 10 for 15mins; turn, and brown other side for about 5mins.

55. Delicious Pesto

Ingredients:
- 1 bunch (80g) fresh basil leaves
- 0.8 oz. (25g) pine nuts
- 1 large clove garlic
- 2.25 oz. (65g) parmesan cheese
- 100ml extra virgin olive oil

Instructions:
1. Toast pine nuts by placing them in the extender kit pan and bake in NuWave oven on 10cm rack for 4mins.
2. Place the basil, pine nuts, garlic and parmesan in the tall cup of the Twister with half of the oil.
3. Fitted with cross blade, blend for a couple of minutes; add the balance of the oil and continue to blend until mixture is smooth.

56. Nuwave Style Chilli Con Carne

Ingredients:
- 17.5 oz. (500g) beef mince
- 7.5 oz. (210g) can red kidney beans; drained
- 1.2 oz. (35g) pkt taco seasoning mix (use half for less spicy)
- 1/4 cup fresh parsley; finely chopped
- 1 tablespoon tomato paste
- 1 egg; lightly whisked
- Salt & pepper to taste
- 2 sheets puff pastry; thawed
- 1/2 cup baby spinach leaves
- 1/4 cup grated tasty cheese
- 1 egg; whisked (for egg wash)
- Sour cream to serve

Instructions:
1. Place mince, beans, seasoning mix, parsley, tomato paste and egg in a large bowl. Season with salt and pepper. Using your hands, mix until well combined.
2. Divide mixture into two equal portions. Spread each pastry sheet with a portion of beef mixture, leaving 2cm border around edges. Top meat on each sheet with half of the spinach leaves and half of the cheese. Roll pastry lengthways to enclose filling.
3. Place seam-side down on chopping board, brush with egg wash and gently cut each roll into 2cm-thick slices.
4. Place slices onto baking paper on 10cm rack.
5. Bake in NuWave oven on 10cm rack; level 10 for 15mins; turn and cook a further 5mins.
6. Serve warm with sour cream.

57. Tasty Pita Crisps

Ingredients:
- Pita bread
- Olive oil
- Sea salt flakes(easily obtained from good supermarkets)

Instructions:
1. Brush oil over both sides of the bread.

2. Sprinkle top-side with salt flakes and cut into wedges.
3. Bake in Nu-Wave oven on 10cm rack for 5 minutes.

Note:
A great snack to serve when having a drink or a much better alternative to potato crisps. To add some difference you may like to add some crushed garlic to the oil or sprinkle your favorite spice mix instead of the salt.

58. Cheese, Bacon & Corn Muffins

Ingredients:
- 1/2 cup polenta
- 1/2 cup milk
- 3 rashers bacon; rindless and chopped finely
- 4 shallots; chopped finely
- 1 1/2 cups self-raising flour
- 1 tablespoon caster sugar
- 11 oz. (310g) can corn kernels; drained
- 4.5 (125g) can creamed corn
- 3.5 oz. (100g) butter; melted
- 2 eggs; beaten lightly
- 1.7 oz. (50g) piece cheddar cheese
- 1/4 cup coarsely grated cheddar cheese

Instructions:
1. Mix polenta and milk in small bowl; cover, stand 20 minutes.
2. Meanwhile; cook bacon, stirring, in heated small non-stick frying pan for 2 minutes. Add shallots and cook, stirring, for another 2 minutes. Remove pan from heat; cool bacon mixture about 5 minutes.
3. Sift flour and sugar into large bowl; stir in corn kernels, creamed corn and bacon mixture. Add melted butter, egg and polenta mixture; mix muffin batter only until just combined.
4. Spoon 1 tablespoon of the batter into each hole of the muffin pan. Cut the piece of cheese into 12 equal pieces, about the size of a 3cm cube; place one piece in the middle of the batter in muffin pan hole. Cover with remaining batter and sprinkle grated cheese over each.
5. Bake in NuWave oven on 5cm rack for 20 minutes until well risen. Turn out onto wire rack. Serve warm.

59. Amazing Mexican Bagels

Ingredients:
- 1 bagel
- 1 tablespoon bottled tomato salsa
- 1/2 small avocado; sliced thickly
- 2 slices cheddar cheese

Instructions:
1. Split bagel in half horizontally.
2. Spread 2 teaspoons of salsa over each bagel half.
3. Top each half with avocado and one cheese slice.

Cook in NuWave oven; on 10cm rack, for 5mins.

Note:
For 2 or more bagels, increase the ingredients accordingly.

60. Delicious Curry Puffs

Ingredients:
- 14 oz. (400g) beef mince
- 1/4 cup tomato sauce (I use spaghetti sauce)
- 1 oz. (30g) butter
- 1/2 cup water
- 1 clove garlic
- 1 tablespoon fruit chutney
- 1 large onion; chopped
- Salt and Pepper
- 1/4 teaspoon chilli powder
- 1 Egg yolk
- 1/2 teaspoon ground ginger
- 1 tablespoon water; extra
- 1/2 teaspoon turmeric
- 3-4 sheets puff pastry; thawed
- 2 teaspoon curry powder
- 1/2 teaspoon paprika

Instructions:
1. Heat butter in pan, add meat, onion and crushed garlic. Cook, stirring, until meat is golden brown; pushing meat with fork so that there are no hard lumps; pour off any surplus fat.
2. Add chilli powder, ginger, turmeric, paprika, curry powder, tomato sauce, water, and fruit chutney. Season with salt and pepper; mix well. Simmer gently, uncovered, for 15mins or until mixture is very thick. Cool completely.
3. Cut pastry sheets into 8cm rounds with pastry cutter. Brush each round with combined egg-yolk and extra water.
4. Place a teaspoonoonful of mixture on each round; fold to form a half-circle. Press edges together firmly. Brush tops with egg mixture.
5. Bake in NuWave oven on 10cm rack; level 10 for 10mins; turn and cook a further 4mins or until pastry is puffed and golden brown.

61. Cashew and Capsicum Pesto

Ingredients:
- 3/4 cup red capsicum; roasted in NuWave oven, skin removed
- 1/3 cup dry-roasted cashew nuts
- 2 cloves garlic; chopped
- 2 tablespoon fresh oregano leaves
- 2 tablespoon olive oil
- 1/3 cup parmesan cheese; finely grated

Instructions:
1. Place all ingredients; except parmesan cheese, into large cup of NuWave Twister.
2. Process by pulsating (turning on and off in spurts), scraping down sides as needed; until smooth.
3. Transfer to a bowl; add parmesan, season with salt and pepper and stir to combine.

62. Delicious Savory Muffins

Ingredients:
- 1 1/4 cup self-raising flour
- 2.3 oz. (65g) butter; melted
- 1 egg; lightly beaten
- 1/2 cup buttermilk
- 1/2 teaspoon paprika
- 2 rashers crispy bacon; chopped
- 1/2 cup grated cheese
- 1/2 cup diced tomato; seeded

Instructions:
1. Sift flour into bowl.
2. Add melted butter, egg, milk and paprika and mix well.
3. Add bacon, cheese and tomato; stir into mixture.
4. 3/4 fill silicone muffin cups or greased muffin pan and bake in NuWave oven on 2cm rack; HI for 20mins. Serve warm.

63. Amazing Chicken, Tarragon and Leek Pie

Ingredients:
- 1.8 oz. (50g) butter
- 3 tablespoons plain flour
- 1 leek; trimmed & thinly sliced
- 1 1/2 cups chicken stock
- 1/2 cup pouring cream
- 1 teaspoon dried tarragon
- 1 pinch white pepper
- Salt to taste
- 1 whole cooked chicken*; deboned, meat chopped
- 2 sheets frozen puff pastry; thawed
- 1 egg; lightly whisked

Instructions:
1. Melt butter in a saucepan over low heat until foaming. Add leek and cook, stirring until leek softens (around 5min).
2. Add flour, stirring, for a further 3 minutes or until mixture bubbles. Remove from heat.
3. Gradually add stock, whisking until smooth. Return pan to heat and cook, stirring until mixture boils and thickens. Remove from heat.
4. Whisk cream, tarragon and pepper into the flour mixture and season with salt. Stir in chopped chicken and set aside to cool completely.
5. Pour chicken mixture into pie dish.
6. Brush edge of pie dish with egg and top pie with puff pastry. Trim edge leaving 1.5 – 2cm overhang. Brush edge with egg. Cut 3cm wide strips of pastry from extra sheet and place on top of pie around outside edge. Pinch both layers of pastry together with fingers**. Cut three slits in top pastry. With leftover pastry cut out leaves and decorate top of pie and brush whole top with egg.
7. Bake in NuWave oven, on 5cm rack for 30mins or until pastry is golden brown.

Note:
A barbeque chicken can be used for this recipe, however you can cook a chicken in your NuWave oven just as easily and this is more cost effective!

Note:
Join pastry by pinching. To do this, take index finger and thumb of left hand and place about 2cm from outer edge of pie, (this hand should be pointing to outside edge). Take index finger of right hand and pointing toward center of pie push outside edge of pie between the fingers of the left hand.

POULTRY RECIPES

64. Delicious Crispy Honey Crusted and Ginger Chicken

Ingredients:
- 2 (4-ounce) skinless and boneless chicken breasts
- 1/2 tablespoon orange juice
- 1/2 tablespoon honey
- 1/4 teaspoon ground ginger
- Dash red pepper flakes (optional)
- 1/8 teaspoon black pepper
- 1/4 teaspoon dried parsley flakes
- 1/2 cup crushed corn flakes

Instructions:
1. Grease a shallow 10-inch baking dish with some melted butter or spray some cooking spray in it to grease it.
2. Combine honey, ginger, red pepper flakes, orange juice and black pepper together in a small mixing bowl. Whisk well until well combined.
3. Use a pastry brush and brush the prepared marinade over the chicken breasts.
4. Mix together the parsley and corn flakes together and roll the marinated chicken breasts in it.
5. Place the corn flake covered chicken breasts in the prepared baking dish and place the baking dish on the 3-inch rack.
6. Bake the chicken breasts on the 'HI' setting for about 15 minutes on each side.
7. Once the juices run clear, the chicken is done.
8. Let it rest for a few minutes before slicing it.
9. Serve with a side of roasted vegetables and mashed potatoes.

Tips:
1. If you are using frozen chicken breasts, increase the cooking time to about 17 to 20 minutes per side.
2. If your chicken breast is smaller, it will cook faster, while a thicker chicken breast will take longer to cook.

65. Tasty Spicy & Sweet BBQ Chicken

Ingredients:
- 1/2 teaspoon hot sauce
- 1/4 cup light brown sugar
- 3 tablespoons cider vinegar
- 2 tablespoons molasses
- 2 garlic cloves; minced
- 1 1/2 tablespoons Dijon mustard
- 1/4 cup ketchup
- 1/2 tablespoon vegetable oil plus extra for grates
- 1 small whole (1 1/2-pound) chicken; cut into individual pieces
- Salt; to taste
- Pepper; to taste

Instructions:

1. Combine together the hot sauce, cider vinegar, brown sugar, molasses, Dijon mustard, minced garlic cloves and ketchup together in a shallow ovenproof baking dish.
2. Place this dish on a 1-inch rack and bake on the 'HI' setting for about 8 to 10 minutes.
3. Place the chicken pieces in a large mixing bowl and pour the prepared sauce over it. Toss well until all the pieces of the chicken are well coated by the sauce.
4. Place the marinated chicken pieces on a 3-inch rack with their skin sides down. Bake on the 'HI' setting for about 13 to 15 minutes.
5. Flip over the chicken and baste the chicken pieces with the extra sauce.
6. Place the chicken pieces; now skin side up, on a 3-inch rack.
7. Bake on the 'HI' setting for another 13 to 15 minutes or until a thermometer inserted in the chicken reads about 165 degrees Fahrenheit.
8. Serve hot with a side of your favorite salad.

66. Cheese Filled Crunchy Chicken

Ingredients:
- 4 boneless chicken breasts
- 3 oz. (90g) cheddar cheese
- 1 tablespoon Dijon mustard
- 1 cup crushed corn flakes
- 1 teaspoon dried parsley flakes
- 1/2 cup buttermilk

Instructions:
1. Cut a deep 5cm long slit in the side of the meaty portion of the breast.
2. Slice cheese into 4 portions and brush with mustard. Place 1 piece of cheese into each slit and secure with wooden toothpicks.
3. Combine cereal, seasoning and parsley.
4. Dip chicken into buttermilk and roll in cereal mixture.
5. Place chicken on baking paper on 10cm rack and bake in NuWave oven on power level HI for 30 minutes; turn over 1/2 way thru to evenly brown.

Note:
Replace cheese with low fat, and buttermilk with non fat, for a healthier option of this recipe!

67. Italian style Rubbed Turkey

Ingredients:
- 1 (5 to 8 pound) turkey
- 1 tablespoon dry rub
- 1 tablespoon Italian seasoning
- Salt; to taste
- 1/8 cup olive oil
- Freshly ground black pepper; to taste

Instructions:
1. Combine the dry rub and Italian seasoning together in a small mixing bowl.
2. Pour the olive oil over the turkey and pour the prepared seasoning over it.
3. Rub the seasoning into the turkey meat.
4. Place the spice rubbed turkey with on the 11-inch cooking rack with its breast side down.
5. Add the Extender Ring to the base tray if required.

6. Cook for about 12 minutes per pound, pausing around the halfway mark to flip the turkey over at 375 degrees Fahrenheit. And Serve hot.

68. Cheesy Turkey Burgers

Ingredients:

- ½ pound ground turkey
- ½ garlic clove; finely minced
- ½ lemon; zested and juiced
- 1 scallion or green onion; finely sliced
- ½ teaspoon black pepper
- ½ egg; lightly beaten
- ½ teaspoon kosher salt
- ¼-cup Japanese Panko breadcrumbs
- ½ tablespoon extra-virgin olive oil
- 2 whole grain buns
- 1 (6 ounce) goat cheese log; cut into 1/2-inch slices

Instructions:

1. Place the turkey, lemon juice, scallions, salt, olive oil, lemon zest, garlic, egg, pepper and breadcrumbs together in a large mixing bowl.
2. Mix well until all the ingredients are well incorporated.
3. Divide the turkey mixture into two equal halves.
4. Form each half into a patty that is about 1-inch thick.
5. Set the patties aside and let the meat rest.
6. Slice the buns into two halves and place all 4 pieces on the 1-inch cooking rack.
7. Cook on the HI power setting for about 5 to 6 minutes or until the buns are well toasted.
8. Remove the toasted buns from the oven and keep aside.
9. Cover the cooking rack with a foil and spray the foil with some cooking spray.
10. Place the prepared turkey patties on the foil.
11. Cook on the HI power setting for about 8 minutes.
12. Turn the patties over and continue cooking on the HI power setting for another 4 minutes.
13. Divide the goat cheese into two equal portions and sprinkle it over the patties.
14. Continue cooking on the HI setting for another 4 minutes or until the cheese is melted enough to spread.
15. Place the turkey patties with their cheese side up on the toasted bun bottom.
16. Top with the top bun.
17. Serve hot with a side of freshly fried French fries.

69. Roasted Chicken and Onions

Ingredients:

- 2 chicken breasts; bone in; skin on
- ½ tablespoon olive oil
- 1 tablespoon Dijon mustard
- ¼-yellow onion; sliced
- 2 sprigs parsley leaves; chopped
- ¼-cup low sodium chicken stock
- 1 teaspoon garlic; chopped
- ½ teaspoon red chili flakes
- ½ teaspoon sugar
- ½ teaspoon black pepper
- 1 teaspoon salt

Instructions:
1. Combine the olive oil, Dijon mustard, parsley leaves, low sodium chicken stock, garlic, red chili flakes, sugar, black pepper and salt together in a large mixing bowl. Whisk well until well combined.
2. Once the ingredients are emulsified, add the onion and chicken to the bowl.
3. Toss the chicken and onion well until they are completely coated with the marinade.
4. Cover the bowl with some cling wrap.
5. Refrigerate the chicken for about an hour or two.
6. Place the chicken with its skin side down on the 4-inch cooking rack.
7. Cook on the HI power setting for about 8 to 10 minutes on each side.
8. Once the chicken is done; rest it for about 5 minutes before slicing.
9. Serve over a bed of wild rice or roasted sweet potatoes.

70. Creamy Chicken Breasts with Bell Peppers and Mushrooms

Ingredients:
- 2 (4 – 6-ounce) chicken breasts
- 1 bell pepper; cut into 1-inch pieces
- 4 large mushrooms; thinly sliced
- 1 cup sour cream
- Salt; to taste
- Pepper; to taste

Instructions:
1. Place the chicken breasts in an ovenproof baking dish.
2. Add in the mushroom slices and bell pepper pieces around the chicken breasts.
3. Pour the sour cream over the ingredients and spread it in an even layer on all the ingredients using the back of a spoon.
4. Season to taste with salt and pepper.
5. Place the baking dish on a 3-inch rack and cook on the 'HI' setting for about 13 to 15 minutes.
6. Flip the chicken breast over and continue cooking for another 13 to 15 minutes.
7. Place the chicken breast on a serving plate and serve hot with a side of sour cream covered mushrooms and bell peppers.

Note:
1. If the chicken breasts you are using are frozen, increase the cooking time to about 15 to 17 minutes per side.
2. The cooking times given in this recipe are approximate. Actual cooking times may vary according to the size and thickness of the chicken breast you are using.

71. Delicious Chicken Parmesan

Ingredients:
- 4 x (180g) boneless/skinless chicken breasts – FROZEN
- Italian dressing
- Seasoned bread crumbs
- 2 ½ cup (250g) grated pizza cheese
- Grated parmesan to taste
- 1/2 cup pasta sauce

Instructions:
1. Combine seasoned breadcrumbs with grated parmesan.
2. Dip chicken pieces in Italian dressing and roll in bread crumbs.
3. Place on 10cm rack and NuWave 13mins per side (or until done).
4. Open oven and spoon sauce on each piece and sprinkle with cheese.
5. NuWave for 2-3 minutes until cheese is golden.
6. Remove chicken from oven and allow chicken to rest for about 5-10 minutes before cutting.

Note:
For a low-cal version try using low-fat Italian dressing and light mozzarella in place of the pizza cheese – both versions will delight!

72. Cilantro and Lime Chicken

Ingredients:
- 2 tablespoon honey
- 4 cloves garlic
- ½ teaspoon oregano
- ½ teaspoon black pepper
- ½-cup red onion
- 1 teaspoon salt
- 8 limes; juiced
- 1 cup fresh cilantro
- 2/3 cup canola oil
- 6 (6-ounce) chicken breasts

Instructions:
1. In the jar of the blender, add honey, garlic, oregano, black pepper, red onion, salt, lime juice, cilantro and canola oil together.
2. Blitz until the mix is well emulsified.
3. Place the chicken breasts in a large sealable bag and pour the marinade into the bag.
4. Seal the bag and toss well until the chicken pieces are well coated in the marinade.
5. Refrigerate the marinated chicken overnight.
6. Remove the chicken breast from the marinade and shake of the excess marinade. Reserve the extra marinade.
7. Place the chicken breasts on the 3-inch cooking rack and cook for about 11 to 13 minutes at 350 degrees Fahrenheit.
8. Turn the chicken breasts over and brush the remaining marinade over them.
9. Continue cooking at 350 degrees Fahrenheit for another 11 to 13 minutes.
10. Remove the chicken breasts from the oven and rest for a few minutes before slicing.
11. Serve hot with the condiment of your choice.

73. Tasty Fried Chicken

Ingredients:
- 1/4 cup buttermilk
- 2 cloves garlic; minced
- 1/2 tablespoon Dijon mustard
- 1/2 teaspoon hot sauce
- 1/4 cup all-purpose flour
- 1 1/2 -2 pounds fresh chicken; cut into thighs, breast legs, and wings, skin removed

- 3/4 teaspoons paprika
- 1/2 teaspoon baking powder
- 1/2 teaspoon dried thyme
- 1/4 teaspoon salt (optional)
- Non-stick cooking spray
- 1/4 teaspoon pepper to taste

Instructions:
1. Place the butter, garlic, mustard and hot sauce together in a small mixing bowl. Whisk well using a wire whisk until well blended.
2. Place the chicken pieces in a shallow glass-baking dish and pour the prepared butter mix over them. Using your hands, repeatedly turn the pieces over and over until all the pieces of chicken are well coated.
3. Cover the baking dish with a cling wrap and refrigerate for at least 3 to 8 hours.
4. In a large sized sealable plastic bag, add the flour, thyme, salt, paprika, baking powder and pepper.
5. Lightly tap the chicken pieces to remove the extra marinade and place the marinated chicken pieces, two at a time; in the plastic bag.
6. Seal the plastic bag and shake the bag to coat the chicken pieces.
7. Lightly tap the chicken pieces to remove the excess flour from the chicken pieces.
8. Place the flour coated chicken pieces on a 3-inch rack and grill on the 'HI' setting for about 15 to 17 minutes on each side.
9. Once the chicken is done; remove it from the oven and let it rest for about 5 minutes before serving.
10. Serve hot with the condiment of your choice.

Note:
If you do not have buttermilk available on hand; use milk with a teaspoon of vinegar added to it for every quart.

74. Tasty Chicken Parmesan

Ingredients:
- 2 (5-ounce) chicken breasts
- 1/2 cup seasoned panko breadcrumbs
- 2 eggs
- 1/2 cup flour
- 1/4 tablespoon pepper
- 1/2 tablespoon kosher salt
- 1/2 (14-ounce) jar marinara sauce
- 2 slices provolone cheese

Instructions:
1. Crack open the eggs in a shallow bowl and lightly season it with salt and pepper. Whisk well.
2. Place the flour in another shallow plate and season it to taste.
3. Finally; place the seasoned panko breadcrumbs in another shallow flat plate.
4. Make light indentions on the chicken breasts with a sharp knife, making sure that you don't cut through.
5. Dip the chicken breasts into the seasoned flour.
6. Then dip the flour coated chicken into the eggs.

7. Finally dip the flour and egg coated chicken into the plate with the breadcrumbs and lightly press until the breadcrumbs stick to the chicken breasts.
8. Place the breadcrumb encrusted chicken on a 3-inch rack and back on the 'HI' setting for about 15 to 17 minutes per side.
9. Place a slice of provolone on each chicken breast and continue baking on the 'HI' setting for another 2 to 3 minutes; or until the cheese melts.
10. Place the chicken breasts on serving plates and slather the marinara sauce over them. Serve hot.

75. Delicious Grilled Cilantro and Garlic Chicken Breasts

Ingredients:
- 3 (6-ounce) chicken breasts; skinless and boneless
- 1/2 small onion; peeled
- 2 cloves garlic; peeled
- 1/2 cup loosely packed fresh cilantro leaves
- 1/2 tablespoon soy sauce
- 1/2 tablespoon granulated sugar
- 2 tablespoons lemon or lime juice
- 1/2 teaspoon black pepper

Instructions:
1. Cover a cutting board with a long piece of plastic wrap and tuck the loose ends under the cutting board to keep it taut.
2. Place the chicken breasts on plastic wrap covered board and cover with another sheet of plastic wrap.
3. Using a meat tenderizer flatten the chicken breast until 1/2 an-inch thick.
4. Place the flattened chicken breasts in a large sealable plastic bag.
5. Place the onions, garlic and cilantro in the jar of a blender. Blitz until finely chopped.
6. Slowly add in the lemon juice, soy sauce, sugar and pepper and continue blending until it forms a smooth paste.
7. Pour the prepared sauce into the bag with the chicken breasts.
8. Seal the bag and give it a good shake until all the chicken breast pieces are well coated.
9. Refrigerate for about 2 to 4 hours.
10. Lightly drain the excess marinade from the chicken pieces and place on a 3-inch rack.
11. Grill for about 13 to 15 minutes per side. Flip it over and grill for another 13 to 15 minutes.
12. Once the chicken is done; remove the chicken pieces from the oven and rest the chicken for about 5 minutes before serving.
13. Serve hot with a condiment of your choice.

76. Amazing Almond, Chicken and Bacon Filled Croissants

Ingredients:
- 4 Croissants
- 1/4 chicken; cooked (barbequed is perfect)
- 2 rashers bacon; chopped
- 2 tablespoon slivered almonds
- 1 tablespoon chopped chives
- 1/2 cup sour cream

Instructions:
1. Toast almonds in NuWave oven; 10cm rack for 4 minutes.
2. Remove chicken meat from bones and chop chicken finely.
3. Cook bacon in pan until crisp and drain.
4. Combine chicken; bacon, almonds, chives and sour cream.
5. Fill croissants with mixture and bake in NuWave oven on 10cm rack for 8 minutes; turning after 5mins.

Note:
I use the pan that comes with the extender kit for toasting the nuts – it's perfect!

77. Tasty Corn, Chicken and Cheese Enchiladas

Ingredients:
- 1/2 tablespoon olive oil
- 1/2 onion; finely chopped
- 1 clove garlic
- 1/2 teaspoon paprika
- 7 oz. (200g) chicken mince
- 5.5 oz. (160g) can creamed corn
- 1/2 cup frozen corn kernels
- 1/4 cup chopped fresh parsley
- 1/2 cup grated tasty cheese
- 4 flour tortillas
- 6.8 oz. (190g) jar tomato & capsicum enchilada simmer sauce (or half of a 375g jar)

Instructions:
1. Heat oil in a non-stick frypan. Add onion, garlic and paprika. Cook, stirring occasionally, until onion is soft.
2. Add chicken. Cook, stirring, until chicken has changed colour.
3. Add creamed corn and kernels.
4. Bring to boil. Simmer, stirring occasionally, for about 5 minutes; or until slightly thickened.
5. Stir in parsley and half of the cheese.
6. Divide chicken mixture among tortillas and roll up to enclose filling.
7. Spread a third of the simmer sauce over base of 25cm pan (extender dish is perfect for this). Arrange tortillas side by side over sauce. Pour remaining sauce over top and sprinkle with remaining cheese.
8. Bake in NuWave oven on 5cm rack; level 10 for 20mins. Serve with sour cream and a crisp garden salad.

78. Special Turkey Burgers

Ingredients:

Burger Ingredients:
- ½ large shallot; finely chopped (1/8 cup)
- ¼-teaspoon salt
- 1 tablespoon olive oil
- 1/8 teaspoon black pepper
- 2 ½ - oz. extra-sharp cheddar cheese; cut into 2 slices
- 3/4 pounds ground turkey
- 2 hamburger buns or Kaiser rolls
- Lettuce leaves

Sun Dried Tomato Mayonnaise Ingredients:
- 1/8 cup oil packed sun dried tomatoes; drained
- 1 teaspoon cider vinegar
- ½ tablespoon water
- 1/8 cup mayonnaise
- 1/8 teaspoon salt

Instructions:
1. Place the sun-dried tomatoes, cider vinegar, water, mayonnaise and salt together in the jar of a blender and blitz until well emulsified.
2. Empty the sun dried tomato mayonnaise in a small bowl and cover with a cling wrap. Refrigerate until the burgers are ready.
3. Place the shallots in a small baking dish and place it on the 4-inch cooking rack.
4. Cook the shallots on the HI power setting for about 3 to 5 minutes.
5. Once done, transfer the shallots to a small bowl and season to taste with salt and pepper.
6. Add the shallots to the turkey and mix well until combined.
7. Divide the turkey mix into 4 equal halves and place on a sheet of wax paper.
8. Pat each quarter until about ½ inch thick.
9. Cover two patties with 1 piece of cheese each.
10. Top the cheese covered patties with the leftover patties.
11. Lightly pinch the edges of the two patties so that the cheese is completely sealed inside the meat. This will make you 2 stuffed patties.
12. Place the prepared stuffed patties on the 4-inch cooking rack and cook on the HI power setting for about 7 to 8 minutes on each side or until the internal temperature of the meat reaches about 150 degrees.
13. Slice the burger buns or roll into two halves and toast the buns on the 4-inch cooking rack with their sliced side up for about 4 minutes.
14. Place the toasted bun halves on a serving plate, spread the prepared sun dried tomato mayonnaise on it, place the stuffed patty and top with the top half of the toasted bun.
15. Serve hot with a side of a fresh salad.

79. Grilled Cornish Game Hens with Potatoes and Artichokes

Ingredients:
- 1 tablespoon lemon juice
- 1 tablespoon extra-virgin olive oil
- 2 cloves garlic
- 1/2 teaspoon oregano
- 1/4 teaspoon kosher salt
- 1/2 teaspoon thyme
- 1/4 teaspoon black pepper
- 4 ounces small potatoes; cut into quarters
- 1 can artichoke hearts; drained
- 1 (11/2-pound) Cornish game hen; washed and dried with paper towel

Instructions:
1. Place the lemon juice, extra-virgin olive oil, thyme, black pepper, garlic, oregano and salt together in a small mixing bowl. Whisk using a wire whisk until well combined.
2. Place the drained artichoke hearts and potatoes in a large mixing bowl. Pour the prepared seasoned oil over the potatoes and artichoke hearts and toss vigorously until well coated.
3. Use a slotted spoon to drain the excess marinade off the potatoes and artichokes and set aside.
4. Brush the remaining marinade over the game hen and make sure the wing tips of the game hen are twisted under the back.
5. Place the hen on a 1-inch rack. Place the marinated potatoes and artichokes around the marinated hen.
6. Grill on the 'HI' setting for about 18 to 20 minutes per side (raise the time to about 32 to 25 minutes per side if you are using a frozen bird).
7. Once completely cooked; remove the hen from the oven and rest for about 5 minutes before serving.
8. Using a sharp knife cut the hens from the center into two halves.
9. Serve hot with the grilled potatoes and artichokes on the side.

80. Hot & Spicy Chicken Curry

Ingredients:
- 2 (4 – 6 ounce) chicken breast; cut into bite size pieces
- 1 green bell pepper; small diced
- 2 scallion; cut into 1/2-inch pieces
- 4 cloves garlic; minced
- 2 tablespoon curry powder or paste
- 4 tablespoons fresh ginger; grated
- 1/2 cup sour cream
- Salt; to taste
- 2 teaspoon coriander leaves; chopped
- Freshly ground black pepper; to taste

Instructions:
1. Place the chicken, green pepper, ginger, salt, scallion, garlic, curry and pepper together in a small mixing bowl. Toss well until the chicken pieces are well coated.
2. Place the chicken pieces on a 3-inch rack and grill on the 'HI' setting for about 13 to 15 minutes per side.

3. Remove the chicken pieces from the oven into a small baking dish and add in the sour cream. Mix well.
4. Place the chicken pieces with the gravy in a serving bowl and serve hot topped with the chopped coriander.
5. Serve with a side of flat bread.

81. Quick & Easy BBQ Chicken

Ingredients:

- 1/2 whole fryer chicken (1 thigh piece, 1 breast piece, 1 wing piece and 1 leg)
- 1 tablespoon honey mustard
- 1/2 cup BBQ sauce
- 1/2 tablespoon soy sauce
- 1 clove garlic; minced
- 1/2 tablespoon Worcestershire sauce

Instructions:

1. Wash the chicken pieces under running water to clean them. On a 3-inch rack, place the chicken pieces in a single layer.
2. Combine the honey mustard, BBQ sauce, soy sauce, minced garlic and Worcestershire sauce together in a small mixing bowl. Whisk with a wire whisk until well combined.
3. Brush the prepared sauce over the chicken pieces using a pastry brush; reserving about half for the other side.
4. Set your NuWave oven on the 'HI' setting and grill the chicken for about 12 to 15 minutes per side.
5. When you flip the chicken pieces over; spoon the remaining prepared sauce over the chicken pieces to keep them moist.
6. Once done; remove the chicken from the oven and rest for about 5 minutes before serving.
7. Serve hot with a side of grilled vegetables and mashed potatoes.

82. Thai Chicken With Assorted Vegetables

Ingredients:

- 2 boneless; skinless chicken breasts
- ¼-teaspoon red pepper flakes
- 6 tablespoon Thai sauce
- ½-cup zucchini
- 6 strips red or yellow pepper
- 1 cup yellow squash
- 1 teaspoon olive oil
- Pepper; to taste
- Salt; to taste

Instructions:

1. Place the chicken breasts on the 1-inch or the 4-inch cooking rack.
2. In a small mixing bowl; combine together the red pepper flakes and the Thai sauce.
3. Spoon about half the prepared sauce over the chicken breasts.
4. Cook the chicken for about 8 to 9 minutes on HI power. (Increase the cooking time to 10 minutes if you are using frozen chicken.)

5. Place all the vegetables in a large sealable bag and add in the salt, pepper and olive oil. Seal the bag and toss until well coated.
6. Once the chicken is done; flip it over and spread the remaining sauce over the breast.
7. Place the oil-coated vegetables around the chicken breasts and continue cooking on the HI power for another 8 to 10 minutes. And Serve hot.

83. Roasted Chicken In BBQ Sauce

Ingredients:
- ½ teaspoon hot sauce
- ¼-cup light brown sugar
- 1/6 cup cider vinegar
- 1 ½ tablespoon Dijon mustard
- 1/8 cup molasses
- ¼-cup ketchup
- 2 garlic cloves; minced
- 1 whole (1 ½ pound) chicken; cut into individual pieces
- Salt; to taste
- ½ tablespoon olive oil
- Freshly ground black pepper to taste

Instructions:
1. Combine together the hot sauce, cider vinegar, brown sugar, molasses, Dijon mustard, garlic cloves and ketchup together in an oven safe baking dish.
2. Place the baking dish on the 1-inch cooking rack and cook on the HI power setting for about 8 to 10 minutes.
3. Place the chicken pieces in a large mixing bowl. Pour the olive oil over the pieces and toss well to coat.
4. Pour some barbeque sauce over the oil coated chicken – just enough to coat.
5. Toss well until the chicken is well coated in the sauce.
6. Spray cooking spray over the 4-inch cooking rack.
7. Place the barbeque sauce covered chicken pieces on the rack, with their skin side down and cook on the HI power setting for about 10 to 12 minutes.
8. Remove the chicken from the oven and brush with the remaining barbeque sauce.
9. Return the chicken pieces to the oven, this time skin side up.
10. Continue cooking on the HI power setting for another 10 to 12 minutes or until the internal temperature of the chicken reads about 165 degrees Fahrenheit.
11. Serve hot with a fresh salad on the side.

84. Hot & Delicious Buffalo Chicken Hoagie Roll Sandwiches

Ingredients:
- 1 1/2 tablespoons butter; melted
- 2 hoagie rolls; split cup ranch dressing
- 1/4 cup buffalo style hot sauce; divided
- 1/4 teaspoon Creole seasoning
- 3/4 cups celery; diagonally sliced
- 3/4 cups carrots; matchstick cut
- 2 tablespoons onion; finely chopped
- 1/2 (4-ounce) package Blue cheese; crumbled
- 6 large deli-fried chicken strips (About 1/2 to 3/4 pounds)

Instructions:
1. In a small mixing bowl place the butter and about 1 teaspoon of the hot sauce together. Whisk using a wire whisk or a fork until just combined.
2. Use a pastry brush to brush the cut sides of the hoagie rolls with the prepared hot sauce butter.
3. In a liner pan; arrange the hoagie rolls in a single layer with their cut sides up.
4. In another medium sized mixing bowl, combine the ranch dressing, Creole seasoning and about1 to 1-1/2 teaspoons of hot sauce together.
5. Add in the celery, carrots and onion to the bowl of the dressing and toss well until all the veggies are well coated with the sauce.
6. Place the chicken in the bottom half of the hot sauce butter coated rolls.
7. Pour the remaining hot sauce over the rolls.
8. Spoon the carrot, celery and onion mixture evenly onto the chicken and top with cheese.
9. Cover with the remaining halves of the rolls.
10. Bake on the '8' setting of your NuWave oven for about 12 to 15 minutes.
11. Serve hot with a side of hot sauce.

Note:
If you are not a fan of Blue cheese you can add in some Parmesan cheese, mozzarella cheese or even some Swiss cheese for a change of flavor.

85. Easy Cheese, Chicken and Spinach Pasta Bake

Ingredients:
- 1/2 cooked chicken*
- 7 oz. (200g) pasta (penne; tortiglioni or rigatoni work well)
- 1/2 tablespoon olive oil
- 1 clove garlic
- 1/2 small red onion
- 1 1/8 cup (250g) jar tomato pasta sauce
- 1 cup tasty or pizza cheese
- 1/4 cup (50g) baby spinach leaves
- Pepper & Salt to taste

Instructions:
1. Cook pasta in a large saucepan of boiling salted water until just tender. Drain and return to saucepan.
2. Meanwhile; heat oil in a frypan over medium to high heat. Add garlic and onion, cook, stirring often until onion is tender and transparent (around 4 minutes).
3. Add onion mixture, pasta sauce, chopped chicken meat, half of the cheese and spinach to hot pasta. Season with salt and pepper. Toss gently until well combined.
4. Spoon pasta mixture into a greased pan (I use the dish that comes with the extender kit but a cake pan or casserole dish is fine). Sprinkle top with remaining cheese.
5. Bake in NuWave oven; on 5cm rack for 15mins.

Note:
Barbeque chicken can be used for this recipe; however you can cook a chicken or 2 chicken breasts in your NuWave oven just as easily and this is more cost efficient!

86. Tasty Turkey and Apple Meatloaves

Ingredients:
- 18 oz. (500g) turkey mince
- 1 egg; lightly beaten
- 1 apple; peeled and grated
- 1 onion; finely chopped
- 2 slices bread; diced
- 2 teaspoon olive oil

Instructions:
1. Grease 6 mini-rectangle oven dishes.
2. Mix together turkey mince, grated apple, onion and egg until combined.
3. Divide mixture equally between baking dishes. Smooth tops.
4. In a small bowl toss diced bread with olive oil. Spoon the oiled bread on top of each mini meatloaf.
5. Bake in NuWave oven on 5cm rack; level 10 for 15-20mins or until cooked through.

87. Stuffed Roasted Chicken Breast

Ingredients:
- 1 (6 to 8 ounce) chicken breast (with wing bone attached)
- 1 cup cooled wild rice
- 2 cups water
- 1/8 cup green pumpkin seeds
- 1/8 teaspoon ground cumin
- 1/8 cup dried golden raisins
- Freshly ground black pepper; to taste
- Salt; to taste

Instructions:
1. Extract the tenderloin from the chicken breast.
2. Dice the tenderloin into bite sized pieces and set aside.
3. Pour water into a 1 and half-quart saucepan and heat over a high flame, uncovered, until the water is boiling.
4. Add the wild rice into the water and stir well.
5. Reduce the flame to a medium low and simmer the rice for about an hour or until the rice is tender to touch.
6. Add the pumpkin seeds, cumin, pepper, raisins, salt and diced tenderloin to the rice and mix well.
7. Carefully cut a pocket into the chicken breast and spoon the prepared rice mixture into it.
8. Pour the olive oil over the stuffed chicken breast.
9. Place the stuffed chicken on a 3-inch cooking rack and roast the chicken for about 20 minutes on each side at 375 degrees Fahrenheit.
10. Heat the juices from the pan until well reduced.
11. Pour the reduced juices over the chicken and serve immediately.

88. Chicken Bites with Wasabi Mayonnaise Dipping Sauce

Ingredients:
- 1 1/2 (1-pound) chicken breasts; boneless and skinless cut into 1/2-inch strips; crosswise
- 1/2 teaspoon baking soda
- 1/3 cup white flour
- 1/4 cup Parmesan cheese
- 1/4 teaspoon paprika
- 1/4 teaspoon garlic salt
- 1/4 teaspoon black pepper
- 1 1/2 tablespoons extra-virgin olive oil
- 1/2 egg; slightly beaten
- 1 teaspoon wasabi
- 1/4 cup mayonnaise

Instructions:
1. Grease a 3-inch cooking rack with some melted butter or spray it with some cooking spray.
2. In a large food storage bag, about 1 gallon, add in the baking soda, garlic salt, flour, cheese and paprika.
3. Place the chicken strips in the egg until coated and then place the egg coated chicken strips in the bag with the dry flour mix.
4. Seal the bag shut and shake it up until all the chicken pieces are well coated.
5. Place the flour covered chicken strips on the greases 3-inch rack.
6. Lightly sprinkle olive oil all over the chicken pieces.
7. Bake on the 'HI' setting for about 11 to 13 minutes. Around the halfway mark, flip the chicken pieces over using tongs.
8. Once the chicken is done; rest it for about a minute before serving.
9. To prepare the dipping sauce combine the mayonnaise and wasabi together in a mixing bowl and whisk well until combined.
10. Serve the chicken pieces hot; accompanied by the wasabi mayonnaise dipping sauce.

Note:
1. If you wish for a spicier dipping sauce; increase the quantity of the wasabi you are using.
2. If you do not like wasabi, honey mustard makes a great accompaniment to this dish too!

89. Fresh Turkey Dish

Ingredients:
- 2 slices bacon; thick cut
- ½ large head romaine lettuce
- 2 eggs
- 1/8 cup olive oil
- ½ teaspoon Dijon mustard
- 1 ½ tablespoon red-wine vinegar
- 4 - oz. roasted turkey breast; cut into cubes
- 1 ½ - oz. blue cheese; crumbled
- ½ ripe avocado; pitted, peeled and diced
- 2 plum tomatoes cut into ½ inch dice
- Freshly ground black pepper; to taste
- Salt; to taste

Instructions:

1. Place the eggs on the liner pan on one side of the pan.
2. Place the 4-inch cooking rack on the liner pan. Place the bacon pieces on the side on the opposite side of the eggs.
3. Cook on the HI power setting for about 13 to 15 minutes.
4. While the eggs and bacon are cooking arrange the lettuce leaves on top of each other and roll to form a cylinder.
5. Hold the lettuce cylinder tightly and slice into ¼-inch strips.
6. Place the lettuce strips in a large mixing bowl and season to taste with salt and pepper.
7. Once the eggs and bacon are done; drain the bacon on a paper towel and remove the cooking rack. Be careful, as the cooking rack will be extremely hot.
8. Use oven mitts or oven tongs to transfer the eggs under a stream of cold water or place them in an ice bath.
9. Peel the eggs and set aside until completely cooled.
10. Once the eggs have cooled, chop the drained bacon and eggs into small pieces and keep aside.
11. In a small mixing bowl; whisk together the vinegar, salt, oil, pepper and mustard together. Whisk until all the ingredients are well incorporated.
12. Pour about half of the prepared dressing over the chopped lettuce and toss well until well coated.
13. Place the dressing covered lettuce onto a serving dish.
14. Add the diced bacon, turkey, blue cheese, eggs, avocado and tomatoes over the lettuce, placing each ingredient in one separate section.
15. Season to taste with salt and pepper and pour the remaining dressing over the salad. And Serve immediately.

90. Amazing Roasted Dijon and Herb Encrusted Chicken Breast

Ingredients:
- 2 (5-ounce) chicken breasts, with the bone in and skin on
- 1 tablespoon Dijon mustard
- 1/2 tablespoon olive oil
- 2 sprigs parsley leaves; chopped
- 1 teaspoon garlic; chopped
- 1/2 teaspoon sugar
- 1/2 teaspoon red pepper flakes
- 1 teaspoon salt
- 1/2 teaspoon black pepper
- 1/4 yellow onion; sliced

Instructions:
1. Combine together the Dijon mustard, olive oil, chopped parsley leaves, chopped garlic, sugar, red pepper flakes, salt, black pepper and sliced yellow onion together in a mixing bowl.
2. Add the chicken breasts to the prepared marinade and toss well until the chicken breasts are well coated.
3. Place the chicken breasts in an airtight container or a sealable bag and pour the leftover marinade over them.
4. Seal the container or the bag and give it a vigorous shake.

5. Refrigerate for at least 4 to 6 hours.
6. Place the marinated chicken breasts on a 3-inch rack with its skin side down.
7. Bake the chicken breasts for about 13 to 15 minutes on the 'HI' setting.
8. Flip it over and cook for another 13 to 15 minutes; and spoon some of the leftover over the chicken breasts.
9. Once cooked through; let the chicken breasts rest for about 5 minutes.
10. Serve hot over some mashed potatoes or over a bed of steamed rice.

91. Tasty Italian Style Chicken

Ingredients:
- 4 large cloves garlic; minced
- 8 tablespoons olive oil; divided
- 1 teaspoon cracked black pepper salt
- 1 teaspoon kosher salt
- 1 (3-pound) whole chicken
- 2 tablespoons chopped thyme
- 2 tablespoons chopped rosemary
- 2 tablespoons chopped oregano

Instructions:
1. Combine about 2 tablespoons of olive oil, pepper and salt together in a small mixing bowl. Pour it over the chicken and rub it in using your fingers.
2. Run a thin spatula handle or a chopstick between the flesh and the flesh of the chicken.
3. Combine the remaining olive oil, rosemary, thyme, garlic and oregano together in a small mixing bowl.
4. Lightly pour this herbed oil between the flesh of the chicken and the skin of the chicken. Rub the herbed oil lightly so that it reaches all the parts of the chicken.
5. Place the chicken on the 1-inch rack breast down. Bake the chicken on the 'HI' setting for about 30 to 45 minutes.
6. Flip the chicken over and spoon the juices from the liner pan over the chicken in order to baste it.
7. Continue baking the chicken on the 'HI' setting for an additional 30 to 45 minutes.
8. Once done, let the chicken rest for a few minutes before carving it.
9. Serve hot with a side of grilled vegetables of your choice.

92. Yummy Chicken Wraps

Ingredients:
- 1 tablespoon olive oil
- ½ onion; julienned
- 4 raw chicken tenders; sliced in half
- ¼-teaspoon salt
- ¼-teaspoon cumin
- ¼-teaspoon pepper
- ¼-teaspoon paprika
- ½ yellow bell pepper; julienned
- ¼-teaspoon garlic powder
- ½ orange bell pepper; julienned
- 2 flour tortillas
- ½ red bell pepper; julienned

Instructions:
1. Pour the olive oil into the liner pan of the NuWave oven.

2. Place the chicken tenders and onions in the liner pan.
3. Sprinkle the salt, cumin, garlic, pepper and paprika over the chicken tenders and onions.
4. Cook the chicken and onions at 400 degrees Fahrenheit for about 5 to 7 minutes.
5. Add the yellow bell pepper and orange bell pepper into the liner pan and mix well.
6. Cook for another 5 to 7 minutes at 400 degrees Fahrenheit.
7. Place the tortillas on a flat working surface.
8. Spoon the prepared chicken and vegetable mix over the tortillas.
9. Roll into a tight roll.
10. Slice at an angle and serve immediately with the condiments of your choice.

93. Cheering Chicken in Amazing Alfredo Sauce Rolls

Ingredients for the Rolls:
- 1/2 tablespoon olive oil
- 1/2 (8-ounce) package cream cheese; room temperature
- 1/2 skinless and boneless chicken breast
- 2 tablespoons freshly grated Parmesan cheese
- 1/4 teaspoon garlic powder
- 1 tablespoon chopped chives
- Kosher salt; to taste
- 1/2 (8-ounce) tube crescent rolls
- Freshly ground black pepper to taste
- 1/4 cup Italian style breadcrumbs

Ingredients for the Sauce:
- 1/2 tablespoon unsalted butter
- 1/4 cup milk
- 1/2 tablespoon all-purpose flour
- Kosher salt; to taste
- 1/4 cup Parmesan cheese or to taste
- Freshly ground black pepper; to taste

Directions for the Rolls:
1. Season the chicken breast with some salt and pepper.
2. Place the seasoned chicken breast on the 3-inch rack.
3. Bake the chicken breast on the 'HI' setting for 12 to 15 minutes per side.
4. Remove the chicken breast from the rack and cool to room temperature. Once cooled; shred the chicken using two forks.
5. Place the shredded chicken, Parmesan cheese, garlic powder, pepper, cream cheese, chives and pepper together in a large mixing bowl. Mix well until well combined.
6. Remove the crescent rolls from the tube and cut into 4 triangles.
7. Place about a tablespoon of the prepared chicken mix onto the triangle and roll up the triangle, starting from the wide end and tuck in the edges beneath the filling.
8. Place the breadcrumbs in a flat plate and roll each triangle in the breadcrumbs. Press lightly so that the breadcrumbs stick to the rolls.
9. Place the breadcrumb-coated rolls in the liner pan with the seam side down.
10. Bake on the 'HI' setting for about 12 to 15 minutes or until the rolls turn golden brown.

Directions for the Sauce:
1. Place butter in a large 1-quart saucepan and heat over a medium low flame until the butter melts.
2. Add the flour to the melted butter and whisk using a wire whisk, until the flour turns light brown.
3. Slowly; add the milk into the flour and cook for about 5 to 7 minutes, whisking vigorously and continuously until the sauce slightly thickens.
4. Season to taste with salt and pepper.
5. Add in the cheese, about 1/2 cup at a time and mix well until smooth.
6. Place the rolls in a serving plate and top with the hot sauce.
7. Serve immediately.

94. Chicken Nugget Casserole

Ingredients:
- ½ (13-½ ounce) package frozen chicken nuggets
- ½ (26 ½ ounce) can spaghetti sauce
- 3 tablespoon grated Parmesan cheese
- ½ teaspoon Italian seasoning
- ½-cup shredded Mozzarella cheese

Instructions:
1. Grease an 8-inch by 8-inch baking dish with some butter.
2. Place the chicken nuggets in the greased baking dish in a single layer.
3. Sprinkle a layer of the Parmesan cheese over it.
4. Pour the spaghetti sauce over the Parmesan.
5. Top with the mozzarella cheese and Italian seasoning.
6. Place the baking dish on the 1-inch cooking rack and cook on the HI power setting for about 10 minutes.
7. Cover the baking dish with a foil and continue cooking for another 5 minutes. And Serve hot.

BEEF & LAMB RECIPES

95. Amazingly Easy Cottage Pie

Ingredients:

- 1.6 Pound (750g) beef mince
- 1 packet French onion soup mix
- 1/2 cup water
- 2 cups frozen peas & corn (or 1 cup peas & corn + 1 cup mixed veg)
- 1 tablespoon Worcestershire sauce
- 1 tablespoon tomato sauce
- 1 teaspoon soy sauce
- 1 tablespoon plain flour (mixed to a loose paste with a little water)

Topping

- 3 – 4 cups mashed potato

OR

- 2 cups mashed potato and
- 2 cups mashed kumara

Instructions:

1. Brown mince in frypan; add soup mix and water. Stir.
2. Simmer on low heat until meat is tender (add a little more water if necessary).
3. Add remaining ingredients; and stir until thick.
4. Pour into pan (the one that comes with the extender kit) or shallow casserole dish.
5. Top with mashed potato and dot with butter. If using both potato and kumara try piping alternate stripes – looks great.
6. Bake in NuWave oven on 5cm rack; level 10 for 25 mins or until golden brown.

96. Delicious and Cheesy Beef Burgers

Ingredients:

- 1/2-pound lean ground beef
- 1/2 egg; beaten
- 1/2 tablespoon Worcestershire sauce
- 1/4 cup dry breadcrumbs
- 2 hamburger buns
- 1/4 package dry onion soup mix
- 2 slices American cheese

Instructions:

1. In a large mixing bowl; place the ground beef.
2. Pour in the beaten egg and Worcestershire sauce.
3. Add in the onion mix and breadcrumbs.
4. Dampen your hands with cold water and lightly mix until all the ingredients are well incorporated. Do not over mix or else your burger patties will be extremely tough.
5. Divide the prepared meat into 2 equal halves.
6. Lightly dampen your hands and shape the meat portions into two round patties, about 1/4 of an-inch thick.

7. Place the prepared beef patties on the 3-inch rack and cook on the 'HI' setting for about 6 to 8 minutes on each side or for about 11 to 13 minutes on each side if you are using frozen patties.
8. Cover the cooked patties with a slice of cheese and cook for another minute or until the cheese melts.
9. Slice the hamburger buns horizontally and place the cheese covered burger patties on the base of the hamburger buns.
10. Cover with condiments of your choice such as lettuce, tomato slices, onion slices, pickle, spiced mayonnaise, mustard, etc.
11. Cover with the top of the bun.
12. Serve hot.

97. Delicious Ancho Chili Spiced Lamb Burgers

Sauce Ingredients:
- 1/2 cup ground ancho chili powder;
- 1/2 tablespoon sour cream
- 1/2 cup water
- 2 tablespoons extra-virgin olive oil
- 1 – 1 1/2 tablespoons fresh lime juice
- 1 small clove garlic; chopped
- Black pepper; to taste
- 1/4 tablespoon salt

Burger Ingredients:
- 1-pound grass-fed ground lamb
- 1/4 teaspoon cumin seeds
- 1/4 teaspoon coriander seeds
- 1/4 teaspoon cayenne powder
- Salt; to taste
- 1 clove minced fresh garlic
- 3/4 teaspoons whole black pepper
- 1 1/2 ounces Cotija cheese
- 3 Ciabatta buns
- Red onion; sliced
- Lettuce or spring green mix
- Tomato; sliced

To Prepare the Sauce:
1. Pour the water into a small saucepan and heat over a medium high flame. Add in the ancho chili powder and continue heating until the water is lightly bubbling.
2. Continue heating until about 1/8th of the total liquid remains.
3. Pour the prepared thickened ancho chili liquid into the jar of a blender.
4. Add in the sour cream, garlic, olive oil and lime juice and blitz until smooth.
5. Season to taste with salt and pepper and keep aside.

To Prepare the Burgers:
1. Place the lamb, coriander, cayenne, salt, pepper, cumin, garlic and pepper together in a large mixing bowl. Mix well until all the ingredients are well incorporated.
2. Divide the mixture into 3 equal parts.
3. Lightly dampen your hands with cold water and form one burger patty from each portion.
4. Place the burger patties on the 3-inch rack. Grill on the 'HI' setting for about 7 to 9 minutes per side.

5. Cut the burger buns horizontally. Spread about a teaspoon of the prepared sauce on the bottom bun.
6. Place the grilled burger patty on the sauce and top with lettuce, onion slices, tomato slices and Cotija cheese.
7. Cover with the top half of the bun and serve hot with a side of crisp French fries.

98. Lamb Chops with a Mint and Red Pepper Sauce

Ingredients:
- 2 (1-inch thick) trimmed shoulder lamb chops
- Coarse salt; to taste
- 1/2 tablespoon dried Italian herbs
- Freshly ground black pepper; to taste
- 1/2 tablespoon olive oil
- 1 1/2 tablespoons fresh lemon juice
- 1 teaspoon Dijon mustard
- 1/4 cup chopped fresh mint
- 3 tablespoons finely chopped red bell pepper

Instructions:
1. Combine he coarse sea salt; dried Italian herbs and black pepper together in a small mixing bowl.
2. Pour the prepared spice rub over the lamb chops and lightly rub until the lamb chops are well coated with the spice rub.
3. Place the spice covered lamb chops on a 3-inch rack.
4. Grill the lamb chops on the 'HI' setting for about 5 to 7 minutes on each side.
5. While the lamb chops cook in the oven; place the olive oil, fresh lemon juice, Dijon mustard, fresh mint and red bell pepper together in a small mixing bowl.
6. Whisk using a wire whisk until well combined.
7. Rest the lamb chops for a few minutes before serving.
8. Serve hot; topped with the prepared mint and pepper sauce.

99. Delicious Andouille & Beef Burgers with Spicy Mayonnaise and Caramelized Onions

Ingredients:
- 1/4-pound Andouille sausage; cut into 1/4-inch cubes
- 1/2 cup pecans; toasted and chopped
- 1/4-pound ground 20% fat beef chuck or ground beef
- 1/2 teaspoon salt
- 1/4-pound sweet onion
- 1/4 teaspoon black pepper
- 1 1/2 tablespoons extra virgin olive oil; divided
- 1/2 teaspoon brown sugar
- 1 1/2 tablespoons garlic cloves; minced
- 1/2 cup mayonnaise
- 1/2 teaspoon Cajun or Creole seasoning blend
- 1/2 tablespoon fresh lemon juice
- 1/4 teaspoon hot pepper sauce

Instructions:
1. Place the Andouille sausage, beef, salt, toasted pecans and black pepper together in a large mixing bowl. Mix well using your hands, until all the ingredients are well incorporated.
2. Lightly dampen your hands and divide the mixture into 3 parts. Shape each part into a 1/2-inch patty each.
3. Place the burger patties in a flat plate and cover with a plastic wrap. Refrigerate while you prepare rest of the ingredients.
4. Place the sweet onion, garlic, 1-tablespoon olive oil and brown sugar together in the bottom of the liner pan.
5. Pop the liner pan into your NuWave oven and roast the onion mixture on the 'HI' setting for about 12 to 15 minutes.
6. Remove the sweet onion mixture from the liner pan and set aside. Make sure you keep the sweet onion mixture warm.
7. Place the burger patties on the 3-inch rack in a single layer.
8. Grill on the 'HI' setting for about 7 to 9 minutes on each side.
9. While the burgers are cooking in the oven; combine together the mayonnaise, Creole seasoning, 1/2 tablespoon olive oil, lemon juice and hot pepper sauce together in a small mixing bowl. Cover with a plastic wrap and refrigerate until you need to use it.
10. Slice the hamburger buns horizontally into halves.
11. Place the grilled burger patty on the bottom half of the bun. Spoon the caramelized onions over the burger patty and spoon the spicy mayonnaise over the caramelized onions.
12. Cover with the top half of the hamburger buns.
13. Serve hot with a side of crisp French fries.

100. Tasty Beef Wellingtons

Ingredients:
- 2 sheets ready made puff pastry
- 7 oz. (200g) or 1 ½ cup duxelles (very finely chopped mushrooms cooked down with onion & seasoning)
- 1.8 oz. (50g) chicken or goose liver pate
- 4 equal portions of eye fillet steak 2.5cm thick

Instructions:
1. Cut the puff pastry in rounds large enough that when meat is placed in center, the pastry is 2.5cm above the top of the meat when drawn up the sides. Cut another round large enough to cover the top of the meat.
2. In center of each large circle of pastry gently spread one quarter of the pate and top with quarter of the mushroom duxelle. Place fillet on top of mushrooms; put small pastry round on top of meat.
3. Brush edges of pastry with egg white, draw pastry up and join to top round – ensure you have a good seal.

4. Bake in NuWave oven on 10cm rack (sprayed with oil) for 10 minutes; turn over and bake for a further 5 minutes or until golden. For well done (no pink) place on 5cm rack and cook for a total of 20 minutes.

Note:

Mushroom Duxelle

For basic duxelles; mince 9 oz. (250g) fresh mushrooms (or mushroom stems) and 1 small onion or 1 to 2 shallots. In a frying pan, sauté the onion or shallot in 1 to 2 tablespoons butter until soft but not brown (3 to 5 minutes). Stir in minced mushrooms, salt and pepper, chopped parsley to taste, and a pinch of tarragon or thyme if you wish.

Depending on your main course, any fresh herb(s) or splash of soy sauce, chicken broth, Madeira, lemon juice, or even fruit, such as dried apricots, can be added. Cook the mixture over medium high heat until the mushrooms give off a lot of liquid; that liquid will evaporate completely (5 to 10 minutes). The duxelles will look like a coarse mash. Cool the mixture slightly and taste for seasoning. This will make about 1-1/2 cups. Duxelles may be frozen for 1 to 2 months.

101. Chuck Roast Beef With Roasted Potatoes

Ingredients:
- ½ onion
- 3 baby gold potatoes
- 2 carrots; washed and peeled
- 1 tablespoon vegetable oil
- Freshly ground black pepper; to taste
- Salt; to taste
- 2 (1 pound) chuck roast
- 1 sprig rosemary
- 1 sprig thyme

Instructions:
1. Coarsely chop the onion and carrots into bite sized pieces. Cut the potatoes into halves.
2. Place the carrots, onion and potatoes in a large mixing bowl.
3. Pour the oil over the vegetables and season to taste with salt and pepper. Toss well until combined. Keep aside.
4. Sprinkle the rosemary, thyme, salt and pepper over the chuck roasts. Rub the seasoning into the chuck roast using your fingers.
5. Place the chuck roasts and the oil coated vegetables on the 1-inch cooking rack.
6. Roast for about 30 to 35 minutes at 375 degrees Fahrenheit for medium rare doneness.
7. Once done to desired doneness, let the roast and veggies rest in the oven for another 5 minutes before transferring the chuck roast to a carving block.
8. Rest the meat for more 5 to 10 minutes before slicing.
9. Serve hot with the roasted vegetables on the side.

102. Tasty Sausages with Bacon and Prunes

Ingredients:
- 4 thick sausages
- 12 pitted prunes
- 2 rashers bacon

Instructions:
1. With a sharp knife; gently make a slit in each sausage being careful not to cut right through.
2. Into each sausage; stuff 3 prunes into slit.
3. Cut each bacon rasher into 2 lengthways and diagonally wrap around sausage and fix with a cocktail stick.
4. Bake in NuWave oven on 10cm rack; level 10 for 15 minutes, turning sausages after 10 minutes.

103. Delicious Veggie and Meat Tortilla Rolls

Ingredients:
- 15 ounces meat of your choice (flank steak or chicken)
- 1/2 green pepper
- 1 medium Spanish onion
- 1/2 red pepper
- 1/2 package fajita or taco seasoning mix
- 1/2 yellow pepper
- 4 ounces shredded Cheddar or Mexican cheese
- 4 ounces ready-made salsa mix
- 1/2 package ready-made tortillas
- Pepper; to taste
- Salt; to taste

Instructions:
1. Slice the meat, green pepper, Spanish onion, red pepper and yellow pepper into 2 slices about 1/4-inch thick each.
2. Sprinkle the taco or fajitas seasoning mix on the meat strips and toss well until well coated.
3. Arrange the vegetables on the outside of a 3-inch rack while placing the meat strips towards the inside.
4. Cook on the 'HI' setting for about 12 to 17 minutes on each side for medium doneness if using flank steak and for about 8 to minutes on each side if using chicken.
5. Place the tortillas in a foil and carefully seal the foil shut.
6. Carefully place the aluminum wrapped tortillas in the liner pan when you open the dome to slip your meats and vegetables over.
7. Once the meat is done cooking; remove the meat and vegetables from the oven.
8. Cautiously unwrap the tortillas from the aluminum foil, making sure that you don't burn yourself.
9. Place the grilled vegetables in a single layer over the warmed tortillas. Layer the cooked meat over the vegetables.
10. Sprinkle a layer of cheese over the meat and top with salsa.
11. Roll the tortillas lightly and serve hot with a salad on the side.

104. Speedy Lamb Meatballs

Ingredients:
- 1/2-pound ground lamb
- 1/4 teaspoon ground cinnamon
- 2 tablespoons finely chopped scallions
- 1/2 teaspoon ground cumin
- 1/2 teaspoon salt
- 1/2 teaspoon ground allspice
- 1/2 egg; beaten
- 1 1/2 tablespoons semolina

Instructions:
1. Place the ground lamb and scallions together in a large mixing bowl. Mix well until well combined.
2. Add in the cinnamon, allspice, semolina, cumin and salt to the meat and scallion mix.
3. Pour the beaten egg over the spice-covered meat and use your hands to lightly knead until you get a semi solid mix. Keep a bowl of cold water handy and constantly wet your palms. This will ensure that the meat doesn't get too sticky to work with.
4. Cover the bowl with a plastic wrap and refrigerate for about an hour or until the meat is firm enough to retain its shape.
5. Divide the meat mixture into 3 parts (about 3 ounces each).
6. Apply oil on your palms and shape each meat portion into a round meatball.
7. Place the meatballs on a 3-inch rack and grill on the 'HI' setting for about 20 to 25 minutes. Pause the oven around the 12-minute mark and turn the meatballs over.
8. Once the meatballs are done; serve hot over a bed of pasta, topped with the sauce of your choice.

105. Roasted Lamb Chops

Ingredients:
- 1 tablespoon olive oil
- ½ tablespoon lemon juice
- 1 garlic clove
- 2 lamb chops; 1-inch thick
- 2 tablespoon chopped ripe tomatoes
- 2 - oz. feta cheese; crumbled
- 2 - 3 pitted Kalamata olives
- Salt; to taste
- ½ tablespoon chopped parsley
- Freshly ground black pepper; to taste

Instructions:
1. Combine together the olive oil, lemon juice and garlic together in a shallow mixing bowl.
2. Add the lamb chops to the bowl and toss well until well coated on all sides. Cover and refrigerate for 30 minutes.
3. In another small mixing bowl; combine together the feta, olives, tomatoes and parsley. Keep aside.
4. Place the marinated lamb chops on the 4-inch cooking rack and sprinkle the pepper and salt over the marinated lamb chops.
5. Roast on the HI power setting for about 14 to 15 minutes. Make sure to turn the chops over around the halfway mark.

6. When the lamb chops are done; divide the feta mixture into two equal parts and spoon it over the lamb chops.
7. Roast on the HI power setting until the cheese melts. And Serve hot.

106. Rosemary and Lamb Cottage Pie

Ingredients:
- 28 oz. (800g) potatoes; peeled and chopped
- 1 tablespoon butter
- 1/4 cup milk
- 1 tablespoon oil
- 1 onion; finely diced
- 2 cloves garlic; chopped
- 17.5 oz. (500g) lamb mince
- 2 carrots; grated
- 2 tablespoon tomato paste
- 1 teaspoon dried rosemary
- 2 tablespoons plain flour
- 1 1/2 cups beef stock
- 1/2 cup grated tasty cheese

Instructions:
1. Place potatoes in saucepan of boiling salted water. Cook for 20 minutes or until tender. Drain; return to saucepan, add butter & milk, mash until smooth.
2. Heat oil in a saucepan over medium heat. Add onions & garlic, cook for 5mins until softened. Add mince & carrot, cook until browned.
3. Add tomato paste & rosemary, cook stirring for 2mins. Remove from heat.
4. Stir in flour. Slowly add stock; stirring after each addition, until combined. Return to heat. Cook for a further 5mins; stirring constantly, until sauce has thickened. Spoon into a 23cm pie dish.
5. Top with mashed potato; then sprinkle over cheese.
6. Bake in NuWave oven; on 10cm rack, for 10-15mins or until golden.

107. Barbeque Lamb Skewers

Ingredients
- 1-pound leg of lamb; fat trimmed and cut into 2-inch cubes
- 1/2 red onion; quartered
- 1/2 large green bell pepper; cored and cut into 4 equal pieces
- 4 large white mushrooms
- Barbeque sauce
- 2 Roma tomatoes; cut in half and seeded

Instructions:
1. Divide the lamb cubes, onion quarters and green pepper pieces into two equal portions.
2. Thread the lamb cubes, onion quarters, green pepper pieces, mushrooms and Roma tomatoes on to bamboo or metal skewers in an alternating pattern of meat and vegetables.
3. Place the prepared skewers on the 3-inch rack and lightly brush the barbeque sauce over them.
4. Grill on the high setting for about 12 to 15 minutes.
5. Flip the skewers over and again brush them with the barbeque sauce.
6. Continue grilling for another 8 to 10 minutes.

7. Serve hot with barbeque sauce on the side.

Tips:
1. You can also add in some chunks of cottage cheese or tofu to the mix.
2. Grill a few pieces of corn on the cob along with the skewers for a delicious accompaniment.

108. Jack O' Peppers

Ingredients:
- 3 bell peppers
- ¼-pound ground beef
- 1 cup wild rice; cooked
- 1/8 cup Italian sausage
- ¼-cup mushrooms; diced
- ½ onion; diced
- 1 tablespoon garlic; minced
- Freshly ground black pepper; to taste
- Salt; to taste

Instructions:
1. Use a sharp knife to carve a jack o' lantern face in the pepper. Slice the top of the pepper and reserve the tops for later.
2. Place the ground beef, wild rice, Italian sausage, mushrooms, onion, garlic, salt and pepper together in a large mixing bowl. Mix well until well combined.
3. Spoon the prepared stuffing into the carved peppers until the jack o' lantern face is completely filled through.
4. Place the peppers on the 3-inch cooking rack.
5. Bake for about 15 to 20 minutes at 350 degrees Fahrenheit.
6. Once the timer is up; place the reserved tops over the peppers.
7. Continue baking at 350 degrees Fahrenheit for another 7 to 10 minutes.
8. Transfer the peppers to the serving dish. And Serve hot.

109. Mustard Coated Leg of Lamb

Ingredients:
- 1 (1 ½ pound) boneless leg of lamb; fat trimmed
- ½ turnip; large diced
- 4 baby Yukon gold potatoes; cut in half
- ½ celery root; large diced
- 2 large carrots; large diced
- 2 parsley roots; leaves removed and roots cut in half lengthwise
- 1 ½ tablespoon extra virgin olive oil; divided
- 2 tablespoon pistachios; roasted and salted
- 1 tablespoon thyme; roughly minced
- 1 tablespoon Dijon mustard
- ½ - oz. rosemary; roughly minced
- 4 garlic cloves; roughly chopped
- Freshly ground black pepper; to taste
- Kosher salt; to taste

Instructions:
1. Place the Yukon potatoes, celery root, carrots, and parsley roots together in a large mixing bowl.

2. Add in the olive oil, black pepper, salt and thyme. Toss well until all the vegetables are coated in oil.
3. Add in the pistachios and transfer the mix to the liner pan.
4. Place the leg of the lamb on a dry and flat working surface.
5. Score the surface of the lamb using a sharp knife.
6. Spread the mustard on the fat side of the leg.
7. Sprinkle the rosemary, black pepper, garlic and salt over the leg of the lamb.
8. Place the seasoned lamb over the vegetables in the liner pan.
9. Cook on the HI setting for an hour or until the internal temperature of the lamb reads about 140 degrees and the vegetables are well browned and tender. And Serve hot.

110. Yummy Cheesy Meatloaf

Ingredients:
- ½-cup carrots; diced
- ½ pound ground chuck
- ½-cup onion; diced
- ½-cup Italian-seasoned bread crumbs
- 1 teaspoon salt
- 1 egg
- ½ teaspoon ground pepper
- 1 tablespoon garlic; minced
- ¼-cup ketchup
- 2 slices provolone cheese; cut into strips

Optional Ingredients:
- Shredded cheese

Instructions:
1. Heat a pan on a medium high flame and add the carrots and onions to it. Cook until the veggies soften.
2. Place the softened carrots and onions, ground beef, egg, pepper, breadcrumbs, salt and garlic together in the bowl of a stand mixer.
3. Mix on the mixer's lowest speed until all the ingredients are properly incorporated.
4. Spray a meat loaf pan with some non-stick cooking spray or grease it with some butter.
5. Pour the meatloaf mix from the bowl into the greased pan. Cover with a cling wrap and refrigerate for an hour.
6. Remove the meatloaf from the pan directly on to the 3-inch cooking rack.
7. Cook for about 20 to 25 minutes at 350 degrees Fahrenheit.
8. Carefully open the dome of your NuWave oven and pour the ketchup over the meatloaf.
9. Cover the ketchup covered meatloaf with slices of the provolone slices and top with the remaining shredded cheese.
10. Continue cooking at 350 degrees Fahrenheit for another 10 to 15 minutes or until the cheese gets a nice brown hue.
11. Serve hot with a side of your favorite condiment.

111. Feta and Tomato Topped Grilled Lamb Chops

Ingredients:
- 1 tablespoon olive oil
- 1/2 tablespoon lemon juice
- 1/2 clove garlic
- 2 (1-inch) lamb chops
- 2 tablespoons chopped ripe tomatoes
- 2 ounces Feta cheese; crumbled
- 2 - 3 Kalamata olives; pitted
- Salt; to taste
- 1/2 tablespoon parsley; chopped
- Freshly ground black pepper; to taste

Instructions:
1. Combine the olive oil; lemon juice and garlic together in a shallow dish.
2. Place the lamb chops in the marinade and turn the lamb chops over and over until all the sides of lamb chops are well coated.
3. Cover the dish with plastic wrap and refrigerate for about 15 to 30 minutes.
4. In another small mixing bowl; combine the Feta, olives, tomato and parsley together. Keep aside.
5. Place the marinated lamb chops on the 3-inch rack. Season with salt and pepper.
6. Grill on the 'HI' setting for about 10 to 12 minutes. Flip the lamb chops over around the 5-minute mark.
7. When timer is up; divide the feta mix into two portions.
8. Top each lamb chop with a portion of the prepared feta cheese mix.
9. Grill on the 'HI' setting for another 3 to 5 minutes or until the cheese melts.
10. Serve hot with a side of your favorite accompaniments.

112. Delicious Mustard and Thyme Crusted Lamb

Ingredients:
- 1 medium boneless leg of lamb (about 2 pounds)
- 1 teaspoon freshly ground pepper
- 1 tablespoon kosher salt
- 2 tablespoon Dijon mustard
- 1 tablespoon chopped thyme
- 2 cloves garlic; finely chopped (about 1 tablespoon)
- 1 tablespoon chopped rosemary
- For Sauce:
- 1 tablespoon granulated sugar; adjust as per taste
- ¼-teaspoon ground pepper
- ½ tablespoon kosher salt
- ½-cup chopped fresh mint
- 1 tablespoon olive oil
- 2 tablespoon white wine vinegar

Instructions:
1. Place the lamb on a clean, dry and flat working surface. Use a sharp knife to trim the extra fat from the lamb and make deep cuts in the thicker parts of the lamb.
2. Cover the lamb with a piece of plastic and use a meat tenderizer to flatten the lamb until it is uniformly thick.
3. Sprinkle generous amounts of salt and pepper on both sides of the lamb.

4. Combine the mustard, thyme, salt, garlic, rosemary and pepper together in a small mixing bowl.
5. Spread the spice rub over the lamb and place the lamb in an oven safe baking dish.
6. Cover the baking dish and refrigerate for a few hours.
7. Roll the lamb into a thick roll and fasten it in place using a kitchen twine. You can also directly place the lamb roll on the 1-inch cooking rack, with its seam side down, without tying it.
8. Roast on the HI power setting for about 18 to 20 minutes per pound of meat for medium doneness.
9. Flip the meat over around the halfway mark.
10. While the lamb roasts, prepare the mint sauce.
11. Pour about 2 tablespoon of water in a medium mixing bowl. Add in the salt, sugar and pepper and whisk well.
12. Add in the mint, oil and vinegar and continue whisking until smooth.
13. Taste and adjust the salt, pepper and sugar according to taste.
14. When the lamb is cooked; rest the lamb for about 10 to 12 minutes before slicing.
15. Serve hot with the prepared mint sauce on the side.

113. Spicy Louisiana Sliders with a Mustard Remoulade Sauce

Ingredients for the Remoulade Sauce:
- 1/4 cup mayonnaise
- 2 tablespoons whole-grain mustard
- 2 tablespoons Dijon mustard
- 1 1/2 tablespoons hot sauce
- 1 scallions; finely diced
- 1 1/2 gherkins; finely diced
- Freshly ground black pepper; to taste
- Kosher salt; to taste

Ingredients for the Burgers:
- 1/2 teaspoon sweet paprika
- 1/4 teaspoon garlic powder
- 1/2 teaspoon dried thyme
- 1/4 teaspoon onion powder
- 1 tablespoon salt
- 1/4 teaspoon cayenne pepper
- 3/4 pounds ground beef chuck
- 1 tablespoon black pepper
- 1/2 tablespoon canola oil
- 4 slider buns; split and lightly toasted
- 8 thin slices pepper jack cheese
- 4 sliced red onion
- 1 tablespoon hot sauce

Instructions:
1. Place the mayonnaise, whole grained mustard, Dijon mustard and hot sauce together in a small mixing bowl. Whisk well until all the ingredients are well incorporated.
2. Add in the scallions and gherkins and mix well. Season well with salt and pepper.
3. Cover the bowl with the sauce with a plastic wrap and refrigerate for about an hour before serving.
4. Combine the sweet paprika, garlic powder, dried thyme, onion powder, salt, cayenne pepper and black pepper together in a small mixing bowl.

5. Lightly dampen your hands and divide the ground beef into 4 parts. Shape each part into a patty and make a light indention in the center of the patty.
6. Spoon about 1/4th of the prepared spice rub on the top of a patty. Lightly rub it in using your fingers. Make sure you do not disturb the shape of the patty.
7. Repeat with the remaining patties.
8. Place the spic rubbed patties on a 3-inch rack with the spiced sides facing down.
9. Sprinkle salt and pepper over the tops of the patties.
10. Grill on the 'HI' setting for about 7 to 8 minutes on each side.
11. Place two sliced of cheese on each patty and continue grilling for another 2 to 3 minutes in the oven or until the cheese melts.
12. To assemble the burgers, place the grilled patties on the lower halves of the buns.
13. Spread the prepared Remoulade sauce on the patties and top with the sliced onions, and pour some hot sauce over them.
14. Serve with a side of crisp French fries.

114. Herb Butter Stuffed Lamb Chops

Ingredients:
- 3 (2-inch) lamb chops
- 2 cloves garlic; minced
- 1/2 stick soft; unsalted butter
- 1/2 tablespoon fresh parsley; chopped
- 1/2 large shallot; chopped
- 1/2 tablespoon fresh tarragon; chopped
- 1/2 teaspoon salt
- 1/4 teaspoon ground black pepper

Instructions:
1. Place the garlic, parsley, shallots, tarragon, pepper and salt together in a small mixing bowl. Mix lightly until combined.
2. Add in the butter and whisk until all the ingredients are well incorporated.
3. Place the lamb chops on a plastic wrap covered cutting board. Cover with another sheet of plastic wrap and lightly hammer the lamb chops with a meat tenderizer until flattened about 1/2-inch thick.
4. Spoon equal amounts of the prepared herb butter onto the lamb chops.
5. Roll the lamb chops and secure into place using toothpicks.
6. Place the prepared stuffed lamb chops on a 3-inch rack.
7. Grill on the 'HI' setting for about 10 to 12 minutes on each side for medium rare done lamb chops. Adjust the cooking time according to your preference.
8. Once done; remove the lamb chops from the oven and rest for about 5 minutes.
9. Serve hot with a side of hot sauce.

115. Quick and Easy Rib Roast

Ingredients:
- 1 (2 1/2 pound) standing rib roast; thawed
- 1/2 teaspoon kosher salt
- 1/2 teaspoon onion powder
- 1/2 teaspoon black pepper

Instructions:
1. Combine the kosher salt, onion powder and black pepper together in a small mixing bowl.
2. Place the standing rib roast on a cutting board.
3. Sprinkle the prepared rub over the rib roast and rub it in using your fingers. Make sure you rub the spice rub in especially around the boney areas.
4. Place the spice rub coated rib roast on a 1-inch rack with its rib side down.
5. Grill on the 'HI' setting for about 14 to 16 minutes per pound of ribs, for rare done ribs.
6. Remove the ribs from the oven and rest them for about 10 minutes before slicing.
7. Serve hot with hot sauce or barbeque sauce on the side.

Tips:
1. For medium rare done ribs; cook the ribs for about 18 to 20 minutes per pound of ribs.
2. For medium cooked ribs; cook the ribs for about 22 to 24 minutes per pound of ribs.
3. For well-done ribs; cook the ribs for about 28 to 30 minutes (or more) per pound of ribs.

116. Bacon, Liver & Onions

Ingredients:
- ½ pound calf liver; 1/2-inch thick
- ¼-teaspoon salt
- ¼-cup milk
- ¼-teaspoon pepper
- 1 medium onion; sliced in to thick rings
- ¼-teaspoon seasoned salt
- 3 - 4 slices of bacon; cut in half

Instructions:
1. Place the liver in a mixing bowl.
2. Add in the milk, pepper, seasoned salt and salt and mix well until all the sides are well coated.
3. Cover and let it rest for an hour.
4. Place the onion rings on the 3-inch cooking rack.
5. Drain the liver from the marinade and shake off the excess marinade. Place the liver on the onion slices.
6. Place the bacon slices on the liver.
7. Cook for about 8 minutes at 350 degrees Fahrenheit.
8. Remove the bacon slices from the liver and flip the liver over. Return the bacon slices and continue cooking at the same temperature for another 8 to 10 minutes.
9. Once done cooking; let the liver rest in the oven (with the dome on) for another 5 to 7 minutes).
10. Serve hot with the bacon and onions.

117. Lamb Burgers With Orange and Olive Salsa

Ingredients:
- 2 2/3 pounds ground lamb
- 2 jalapenos; seeded and minced
- 2 cloves garlic; minced
- 4 tablespoon fresh cilantro; chopped
- 1 ½ teaspoon ground black pepper
- 2 large shallots
- 2 teaspoon salt
- 1 teaspoon ground cumin
- 1 teaspoon paprika
- 8 burger buns; of your choice

Salsa Ingredients:
- 4 tablespoon extra virgin olive oil
- 2 tablespoon honey
- 2 tablespoon fresh lemon juice
- 2 cups chopped red onion
- 4 large oranges; peel and remove pith, cut oranges into ⅓ inch cubes
- ½-cup chopped pitted green olives

Instructions:
1. Place the ground lamb in a large mixing bowl.
2. Add in the jalapenos, garlic, cilantro, ground black pepper, shallots, salt, cumin and paprika.
3. Mix well until all the ingredients are well combined.
4. Divide the lamb mixture into 8 equal parts and flatten to make 1-inch thick patties.
5. Grease the 3-inch cooking rack with some butter or spray it with some cooking spray.
6. Arrange the prepared burger patties in a single layer on the greased 3-inch cooking rack.
7. Cook on the HI power setting or at 400 degrees Fahrenheit for about 5 to 6 minutes per side for medium doneness. Increase the cooking time to about 8 to 10 minutes per side for well-done burgers.
8. In another mixing bowl, combine together the olive oil, honey, fresh lemon juice, red onion, orange cubes and green olives together.
9. Place the patties on the burger buns and spoon the prepared salsa over them. And Serve hot.

118. Delicious Bacon Wrapped Meatloaf

Ingredients:
- 21 oz. (600g) beef mince
- 1 cup breadcrumbs
- 1/2 cup spaghetti sauce
- 2 cloves garlic; minced
- 1/2 medium yellow onion; minced
- 1 tablespoon dry Italian herbs
- 2 large eggs
- 1/4 cup grated Parmesan cheese
- 7 oz. (200g) thinly sliced bacon rashers (I use Thin 'n Crispy)
- Piece of baking paper a little larger than the top of the loaf pan.

Instructions:
1. Spray loaf pan with oil and line pan with bacon rashers leaving extra length hanging over the sides of the pan.
2. Mix together the remaining ingredients.
3. Fill loaf pan with meat mixture and bring ends of bacon rashers into centre to seal.

4. Bake in NuWave oven on 2cm rack; level 10 for 20min.
5. Gently turn meatloaf over onto baking paper (on rack) and remove loaf pan. Cook for a further 30min.

119. Shepherd's Pie

Ingredients:
- ½ tablespoon olive oil
- ½ large onion; grated
- ½ pound ground beef and lamb mix
- 1 large carrot; grated
- 1 tablespoon Worcestershire sauce
- 1 tablespoon tomato paste
- 2 - 3 - oz. red wine
- 2 sprigs rosemary; finely chopped
- 2 sprigs fresh thyme; finely chopped
- ½-cup beef stock
- ½ egg
- 1 ½-cups mashed potatoes; fresh or leftover
- 1 cup parmesan cheese; grated and divided
- Freshly ground black pepper; to taste
- Kosher salt; to taste

Instructions:
1. Pour the olive oil into a 3-quart pot and heat on a high flame until the oil is lightly smoking.
2. Add the grated carrot to the pot and sauté for about 2 to 3 minutes or until the carrot is tender.
3. Add the onions to the pot and mix well. Sauté for about 3 to 4 minutes or until the onion becomes translucent.
4. Add the lamb and beef mix to the pot. Continue cooking for about 10 to 12 minutes or until the meats are well browned.
5. If there is too much fat, drain it.
6. Pour the tomato paste into the pot and cook for about 2 minutes or until the paste is caramelized.
7. Pour in the wine and Worcestershire sauce.
8. Continue heating on the high flame until slightly reduced.
9. Add in the beef stock and continue heating for about 12 to 15 minutes or until the broth thickens into a thick gravy.
10. Season according to taste with salt and pepper and take the pot off the heat.
11. Pour the mixture into a large 10-inch baking pan and cover.
12. Refrigerate for about half an hour.
13. In a mixing bowl; place the mashed potatoes, salt, 1 ½-cup Parmesan cheese, egg and pepper together. Mix well until well combined.
14. Spoon the mashed potato mix over the meat mix and smooth using the back of a spoon.
15. Add the remaining cheese to the top of the pie and place the baking pan on the 1-inch cooking rack.
16. Bake at 400 degrees Fahrenheit for about 15 to 17 minutes or until the top potato is well browned. And Serve hot.

120. Rosemary, Thyme Crusted Lamb Shanks

Ingredients:
- 3 lamb shanks
- 1 clove garlic; crushed
- ½ red onion; chopped
- ½ sprig fresh rosemary
- 1 tablespoon fresh thyme or ½ tablespoon dry
- 1 bay leaf
- ½ tablespoon Worcestershire sauce
- 3/4 cup vegetables stock (broth)
- ½ (14 ounce) can crushed tomatoes
- 1 ½ tablespoon white wine
- ¼-teaspoon pepper
- ¼-teaspoon salt

Instructions:
1. Arrange the lamb shanks in a single layer on the 4-inch cooking rack.
2. Cook on the HI power setting for about 8 minutes on each side or until the desired level of doneness is achieved.
3. Place the roasted lamb shanks in a large mixing bowl.
4. Combine the garlic, onion, rosemary, thyme, bay leaf, Worcestershire sauce, vegetable stock, crushed tomatoes, white wine, pepper and salt together in a small mixing bowl.
5. Pour the prepared marinade over the lamb shanks and toss well until the lamb shanks are well coated.
6. Place the lamb shanks, along with the marinade, in the liner pan.
7. Cook on the 7 power setting for about 3 to 4 hours.
8. Make sure to pause the oven at regular intervals to turn the shanks over to ensure even cooking.
9. Serve hot over a bed of mashed potatoes.

121. Tangy Thai Steak, Peanut Salad and Bean Sprout

Ingredients:

Marinade Ingredients:
- 1/8 cup freshly squeezed lime juice
- ½ tablespoon soy sauce
- 1/8 cup rice wine vinegar
- ½ tablespoon sugar
- 1 ½ tablespoon vegetable oil
- ¼-teaspoon red pepper flakes

Salad Ingredients:
- 1 (1 pound) skirt steak
- Freshly ground black pepper; to taste
- Coarse salt; to taste
- ¼-pound carrots; julienned
- ¼-cup fresh mint leaves
- 1 small head romaine lettuce; cut crosswise into 1-inch ribbons
- 1/6 cup salted peanuts; chopped
- ½-cup fresh bean sprouts

Instructions:
1. Pour the lemon juice, soy sauce, rice wine vinegar and vegetable oil together in the jar of a blender.

2. Add in the sugar and red pepper flakes and blitz until well combined.
3. Sprinkle salt and pepper over the skirt steak and rub it in using your fingers.
4. Place the seasoned steak in a baking dish.
5. Pour about ¼ of the prepared marinade over the steak. Turn the steak over repeatedly, until all the sides of the steak are well coated by the marinade.
6. Reserve the remaining marinade.
7. Cover the baking dish and refrigerate for about 2 to 4 hours.
8. Remove the steak from the marinade and shake off the excess marinade.
9. Place the steak on the 3-inch cooking rack and cook for 6 to 8 minutes on each side at 350 degrees Fahrenheit.
10. Once the steak is cooked to the desired degree of doneness, transfer the steak to the carving board and rest for about 5 to 10 minutes before slicing.
11. While the steak rests, place the carrots, sprouts, lettuce peanuts and mint together in a large mixing bowl.
12. Pour the reserved marinade over the prepared salad and toss well until all the ingredients are well coated.
13. Slice the steak into slices about ¼-inch thick against the grain and then cut the slices into halves in the opposite direction.
14. Spoon the prepared salad onto a serving plate and place the steak slices over the bed of salad. Sprinkle salt and pepper over the steak slices and serve immediately.

122. Stuffed Cabbage Rolls

Ingredients:
- ½ pound cooked corned beef; chopped
- 1 ½ celery stalks; finely chopped
- ½-cup cooked brown rice
- ½ onion; finely chopped
- ½ head green cabbage; blanched
- 1 egg; lightly beaten
- ½-cup beef broth
- Freshly ground black pepper; to taste
- Kosher salt; to taste

Instructions:
1. Place the cooked corned beef and the cooked brown rice together in a large mixing bowl. Mix well until well combined.
2. Add the celery, egg and onion to the mixing bowl. Mix well until well combined.
3. Sprinkle salt and pepper over the beef mixture and mix well.
4. Lay the cabbage leaves on a flat surface and place about 3 tablespoon of the prepared corned beef mixture on each leaf.
5. Roll the leaf up; tucking in the sides as you go.
6. Place the prepared cabbage rolls directly onto the liner pan with the seam side down.
7. Pour the beef broth onto the rolls.
8. Cover the liner pan with some aluminum foil and bake on the HI power setting for about 20 to 25 minutes.
9. Serve hot with the condiment of your choice.

123. Tarragon and Butter Stuffed Lamb Chops

Ingredients:
- 3 (2 inch) lamb chops
- 2 cloves garlic; minced
- ½ stick soft; un-salted butter
- ½ tablespoon fresh parsley; chopped
- ½ large shallot; chopped
- ½ tablespoon fresh tarragon; chopped
- ½ teaspoon salt
- 1/8 teaspoon ground black pepper

Instructions:
1. Place the softened butter in a small mixing bowl.
2. Add in the garlic, parsley, shallot, tarragon, salt, and black pepper. Mix well until all the ingredients are well combined.
3. Spoon the mixture into the lamb pockets and hold them in place using toothpicks.
4. Arrange the lamb chops in a single layer on the 3-inch cooking rack.
5. Cook on the HI setting for about 6 to 7 minutes per side for medium rare done lamb chops. And Serve hot.

124. Sour and Sweet Lamb Chops

Ingredients:
- ½ tablespoon red wine vinegar
- ¼-teaspoon ground sage
- ½ teaspoon dark brown sugar
- ¼-teaspoon garlic powder
- 2 (1-inch thick) lamb chops
- ¼-teaspoon pepper

Instructions:
1. Whisk together the red wine vinegar, ground sage, brown sugar, garlic powder and pepper together in a small mixing bowl.
2. Pour the prepared spice rub over the lamb chops and rub the seasoning into the meat using your fingers.
3. Place the lamb chops on the 4-inch cooking rack.
4. Cook on the HI power setting for about 6 to 8 minutes for medium cooked lamb chops
5. Serve hot with a side of mashed potatoes or roasted vegetables.

125. Tasty Steak Sandwiches

Ingredients:
- 1 (6 ounce) top sirloin steak
- Salt; to taste
- 2 ½ tablespoon olive oil; divided
- Freshly ground black pepper; to taste
- ¼-cup mayonnaise
- 2 French rolls
- 1 tablespoon parsley
- ½ tablespoon garlic

Instructions:
1. Pour about 1-½ tablespoon of the olive oil over the steak and rub the oil on both sides of the steak.

2. Sprinkle the salt and pepper over both the sides of the steak and rub the seasoning into the steak using your fingers.
3. Place the prepared steak on the 4-inch cooking rack and place it in your NuWave oven.
4. Cook for about 6 minutes per side on the HI power setting.
5. Remove the steak from the oven and keep it aside to cool.
6. Cut open the buns and place them on the 4-inch cooking rack.
7. Toast on the HI power setting for about 4 minutes.
8. While the buns are toasting, mix together the mayonnaise, parsley, garlic and the remaining 1-tablespoon olive oil in the jar of a blender. Blitz until all the ingredients emulsify together.
9. Once the steak is well rested, slice it into ¼-inch slices against the grain.
10. Spread the prepared garlic mayonnaise over the toasted bottom buns and place the steak slices over it.
11. Cover with the toasted top buns.
12. Serve immediately with a side of fresh French fries or a fresh salad.

126. Crabmeat Stuffed Beef Roulade

Ingredients:
Roulade Ingredients:
- 1 tablespoon butter
- 4 - oz. crimini mushrooms; sliced
- 1 tablespoon shallots; minced
- 1 tablespoon olive oil
- ¼-pound lump crabmeat; carefully picked over and cartilage removed
- 1/8 cup parsley; minced
- 1/8 cup white wine
- Pinch kosher salt
- ¼-pound fresh spinach; washed and stems removed
- ½ pound bottom or top round; trimmed and butterflied to ½ inch thickness
- Pinch white pepper

Sauce Ingredients:
- ½-cup port wine
- Pinch of salt
- 1 tablespoon unsalted butter
- Pinch of pepper

Instructions:
Instructions for Roulade:
1. Place the butter and olive oil in a large skillet and heat over a medium high flame until the butter has melted and combined with the oil.
2. Add the shallots and onions to the pan and sauté for about 3 to 5 minutes or until the vegetables have softened.
3. Pour the port wine into the pan and cook for another 2 to 3 minutes or until the port wine has completely evaporated.
4. Add the parsley, crabmeat and spinach to the pan and cook for about 4 to 5 minutes or until the edges of the spinach have wilted.
5. Season to taste with salt and pepper and remove the pan off the flame. Let the mix cool to room temperature.

6. Place the beef on a flat work surface and sprinkle salt and pepper over the beef.
7. Lightly squeeze the crabmeat mixture and remove the extra water from it.
8. Place the crabmeat mixture on the seasoned loin and spread the mixture down the center of the loin, leaving about ½ an inch border from around the edges.
9. Start rolling the loin over the crabmeat from the short end tightly.
10. Tie the roll with a kitchen twine at regular 1-inch intervals.
11. Sprinkle salt and white pepper around the outside of the roulade and place the roulade with its seam side down on the 4-inch cooking rack.
12. Roast the roulade on the HI power setting for about 5 to 6 minutes per side and meat is well browned. The internal temperature of the meat should reach 150 degrees Fahrenheit.
13. Remove the roulade from the oven and place on a cutting board, loosely covered with a kitchen towel. Let the roulade rest for about 6 to 7 minutes before slicing it.
14. Slice the roulade into 3/4-inch thick slices and serve hot covered with the prepared port wine sauce.

Instructions for Sauce:
1. In a small stockpot, pour the port wine and heat on a high flame until the port wine is bubbling.
2. Once the port wine is bubbling, reduce the heat so that the port wine is simmering.
3. Simmer until the port wine is reduced to about 1/6 cup.
4. Remove the wine from the heat and add in the butter.
5. Whisk well until well combined.
6. Season to taste with salt and pepper.
7. Keep warm while the roulade cooks.

127. Easy Rib Eye Steak

Ingredients:
Steak Ingredients:
- 1 (12-ounce) rib eye steak
- 1/8 teaspoon kosher salt
- 1/8 teaspoon black pepper
- ¼-tablespoon extra-virgin olive oil

Sweet Potatoes Ingredients:
- 1 large sweet potato
- ½ tablespoon extra-virgin olive oil
- 1 clove garlic; minced
- 1 tablespoon parmesan cheese; grated
- 1/8 teaspoon black pepper
- 1/8 teaspoon kosher salt

Instructions:
Instructions for Steak:
1. Pat the steak lightly with a kitchen towel, until the steak is dry to touch.
2. Sprinkle the salt and pepper over both sides of the steak and rub the seasonings into the meat using your fingers.
3. Pour the olive oil over the steak and rub well.
4. Place the steak on the 1-inch cooking rack.
5. Roast on the HI power setting for about 6 to 7 minutes for medium rare doneness, 8 to 10 minutes for medium doneness and 11 to 13 minutes for a well-done steak.
6. Once done to your desired level of doneness, allow the meat to rest for about 8 to 10 minutes, cover loosely with a piece of foil.

Instructions for Sweet Potatoes:
1. Cut the potatoes into quarters for 4 equal sized wedges.
2. Place the potato wedges in a large mixing bowl and add in the olive oil, garlic, salt and pepper.
3. Toss well to coat the potatoes evenly.
4. Cover the 1-inch cooking rack with a foil and spray it with some cooking spray.
5. Place the oil tossed potato wedges on the foil with their skin sides down.
6. Cook on the HI power setting for about 18 to 20 minutes or until the potatoes are tender and become well browned.
7. Sprinkle the Parmesan over the potato wedges and serve with the steak immediately.

SEAFOODS RECIPES

128. Easy Creamy Tuna Mornay

Ingredients:
- 1 oz. (30g) butter
- 1 medium brown onion (finely chopped)
- 1 trimmed stick celery (chopped finely)
- 1 tablespoon plain flour
- 3/4 cup milk
- 1/2 cup cream
- 1/3 cup grated cheddar cheese
- 4.5 oz. (130g) can corn kernels; drained
- 6.5 oz. (185g) can tuna; drained
- 1/2 cup stale breadcrumbs
- 1/4 cup grated cheddar; extra

Instructions:
1. Melt butter in a frypan on a moderate heat and add onion.
2. Cook for about 3 minutes; add celery and cook another 2 minutes or until celery softens.
3. Add flour to pan and cook for 1 or 2 minutes.
4. Remove pan from heat and gradually add milk and cream, stirring constantly.
5. Return to heat; stirring until mixture boils and thickens.
6. Add cheese; stirring until cheese is melted.
7. Gently fold in corn and tuna.
8. Divide mixture evenly into 2 individual casserole dishes (2 cup capacity).
9. Sprinkle combined breadcrumbs and extra cheese over top.
10. Bake in NuWave oven on 5cm rack; level 10 for 12 – 15 minutes or golden brown and crispy on top.

129. Tangy Lemon Salmon Topped With a Sweet and Spicy Mango Salsa

Ingredients for the Salmon:
- 2 (6-ounce) salmon fillets
- 1/2 tablespoon olive oil
- 1 tablespoon lemon juice
- 1/2 tablespoon grated lemon zest
- 1/4 teaspoon black pepper
- 1 teaspoon Dijon mustard

Ingredients for the Salsa:
- 1/2 ripe mango; peeled and diced
- 2 tablespoons red bell pepper; chopped
- 1 green onion; finely chopped
- 1 tablespoon lime juice
- 1 tablespoon fresh cilantro; chopped

Instructions:
1. Combine the lemon juice, lemon zest, and pepper, olive oil and Dijon mustard together in a small mixing bowl. Whisk well using a wire whisk, until all the ingredients are well incorporated.
2. Place the salmon fillets in a shallow baking dish and pour the prepared marinade over them.
3. Cover with a plastic wrap and let the fish marinate in the refrigerator for about 30 to 45 minutes.

4. While the fish marinates in the refrigerator, prepare the salsa.
5. Place the mango, red bell pepper, green onion and cilantro together in a mixing bowl. Mix well.
6. Pour the lemon juice over the prepared salsa and let it sit for about 5 to 7 minutes before mixing again.
7. Cover with a plastic wrap and refrigerate until you need to use it.
8. Place the marinated salmon fillets on the 3-inch rack.
9. Cook on the 'HI' setting for about 7 to 9 minutes per side.
10. Serve hot topped with the chilled mango salsa.

130. Delicious Soy Salmon

Ingredients:
- 2 fresh salmon fillets; about 2 1/2 cm thick
- 1 tablespoon ketjap manis (a sweet Indonesian soy sauce available from the Asian section of your supermarket)
- 1 tablespoon soy sauce
- 2 tablespoons sweet chilli sauce
- 1 tablespoon fresh ginger; finely grated
- 1 tablespoon lemon or lime juice

Instructions:
1. Mix together ketjap manis, soy sauce, sweet chilli sauce, grated ginger and lemon or lime juice.
2. Coat salmon fillets with sauce mixture and place in NuWave oven on baking paper on 10cm rack.
3. Bake in NuWave oven; 15mins or until cooked through (this will depend on the thickness of the salmon).

131. Easy Nutty Orange Chili Salmon

Ingredients:
- 2 Salmon fillets
- 2 tablespoon orange marmalade
- 1 1/2 teaspoon hot chilli flakes
- 2.6 oz. (75g) dry roasted chopped cashews; peanuts, almonds & pistachios (leave whole) *

Instructions:
1. Combine marmalade, chilli flakes and nuts in a bowl. Mix well.
2. Pack half mixture on skinless side of each salmon fillet.
3. Bake in NuWave oven on 10cm rack; level 10 for 12mins or salmon is cooked through to your liking.

Note:
This mixture of nuts is available in good supermarkets.

132. Quick and Easy Garlic Prawn Rolls

Ingredients:
- 6 small par-baked French bread rolls
- 2.6 oz. (75g) unsalted butter
- 2 cloves garlic; crushed
- 1 tablespoon flat leaf parsley; chopped
- 1/2 kg cooked & peeled small prawns (green prawns can be used – see note below)

Instructions:
1. Make cut lengthways in the top of each bread roll.
2. Melt butter with garlic together; stirring, in a small pan. *
3. Remove from heat and use a pastry brush to brush the insides of the rolls with some of the garlic butter.
4. Add parsley to garlic butter and then stir in prawns.
5. Fill each roll with the prawn mixture and place on 10cm rack.
6. Bake in NuWave oven for 5-6mins. And Serve hot.

Note:
This is a scrumptious dish just perfect for a snack with drinks, a quick and easy lunch with salad or an entrée that will be a big hit!
If using green prawns; add them to the melted garlic butter and cook, stirring until just done.

133. Delicious Baked Lobster Tail With Bacon Mornay

Ingredients:
- 1 lobster tail; meat removed and roughly chopped
- 2 bacon rashers; finely chopped
- 1.5 oz. (40g) butter
- 1 1/2 tablespoon plain flour
- 1 1/2 cups milk
- 1 egg yolk
- 2 tablespoons flat leaf parsley; chopped
- Lemon wedges to serve

Instructions:
1. Heat oil in a frying pan over medium heat; add the lobster and bacon and cook for 4-5 minutes or until lobster is golden and bacon is crispy.
2. Melt butter in a small saucepan over medium heat until foaming. Add flour, cook, stirring, for 1 minute or until bubbling.
3. Remove from heat and slowly add milk, whisking continuously; until mixture is smooth.
4. Return to heat reducing heat to low. Cook, stirring with a wooden spoon; for 3-5 minutes or
5. until sauce comes to the boil. Remove from heat and whisk in egg yolk and season with salt and pepper.
6. Place lobster in a shallow pan (extender kit pan is ideal) and pour sauce over. Top with bacon.
7. Bake in NuWave oven on 10cm rack; level 10 for 5mins or top is golden.
8. Sprinkle with parsley and serve with lemon wedges.

134. Funny Taco Chicken Strips

Ingredients:
- 14 oz. (400g) chicken tenderloins
- 1.2 oz. (35g) packet mild taco seasoning mix
- 1 cup light sour cream
- 7 oz. (200g) plain corn chips; crushed

Instructions:
1. Place seasoning mix and sour cream in a shallow bowl. Stir to combine. Place chips on a plate.
2. Dip 1-piece chicken into seasoning mixture. Coat in chips.
3. Refrigerate for 30 minutes.
4. Spray chicken with spray oil and place on 10cm rack.
5. Bake in NuWave oven for 12 minutes turning over for last couple of minutes.
6. Serve with lemon wedges.

135. Delicious Filo Wrapped Salmon With Greek Yoghurt And Dill Dressing

Ingredients:
- 1 Salmon fillet
- 3 sheets filo pastry (which has been sprayed with canola oil)
- Large dollop of greek yoghurt with fresh dill added

Instructions:
1. Wrap salmon in the filo to make a parcel.
2. Bake in NuWave oven on 10cm rack; level 10 for 8mins; turn and brown other side for about 4mins.
3. Serve with dollop of greek yoghurt with dill and hot chips (can be cooked at the same time)

136. Zingy Roasted Shrimp with a Herbed Salsa

Ingredients for the Shrimp
- 3/4 pounds large shrimp; peeled and deveined
- 3 garlic cloves; thinly sliced
- 1 red Serrano pepper; halved lengthwise
- 1 bay leaf
- 1/2 lemon; cut into wedges
- 1/4 cup olive oil

Ingredients for the Herb Salsa:
- 2 tablespoons fresh cilantro; chopped
- 1/2 tablespoon finely grated lemon zest
- 2 tablespoons fresh flat-leaf parsley; chopped
- 1/2 tablespoon olive oil
- Freshly ground pepper; to taste
- Kosher salt; to taste

Instructions:
1. Place the shrimp and Serrano pepper halves in an ovenproof dish, along with the bay leaf, garlic and olive oil.

2. Mix lightly until all the ingredients are coated with olive oil.
3. Place the baking dish on the 3-inch rack.
4. Cook on the 'HI' setting for about 3 to 5 minutes.
5. While the shrimp cooks; prepare the salsa.
6. Combine the cilantro, lemon zest and parsley together in a small mixing bowl.
7. Season to taste with salt and pepper.
8. Pour the olive oil over the salsa and let it stand for a few minutes before mixing it up.
9. When the shrimp is done; pour in the lemon juice and toss well to coat.
10. Serve the shrimp hot; topped with the prepared salsa.

137. A Medley of Shellfish

Ingredients:
- 2 littleneck clams
- 2 mussels
- 2 large shrimp
- 1 squid; cleaned and cut into 1-inch rings
- 1 tablespoon olive oil
- 1 clove garlic; minced
- 1/2 tablespoon hot sauce
- 2 tablespoons clam juice
- Dash parsley; minced

Instructions:
1. Carefully scrub the mussels and clams until clean.
2. Place the clams, mussels, shrimp, squid rings, olive oil, garlic, hot sauce, clam juice and parsley together in an ovenproof baking dish.
3. Place the baking dish on the 3-inch rack and cook on the 'HI' setting for about 12 to 15 minutes or until all the mussels and clams open up.
4. Serve hot.

Tips:
1. About halfway through the cooking process, pause your oven and carefully extract the baking dish from the oven. Shake it well and return to the oven for cooking. This will help to open up the mussels and clams faster.
2. Do not eat any of the unopened mussels and clams.
3. Do not forget to devein the shrimps and remove the 'poo vein'.

138. Mouth Watering Curried Prawns

Ingredients:
- 1.6 pound (750g) green prawns (shelled)
- 2 oz. (60g) butter
- 1 tablespoon curry powder
- 2 sticks celery; chopped
- 1 large onion; finely diced
- 1/2 green pepper
- 1 medium tomato; peeled and diced
- 4 tablespoon plain flour
- Pepper & Salt to taste
- 1 1/2 cups water
- 1 cup milk
- 2 teaspoon chicken stock powder
- 1 teaspoon sugar
- 1 tablespoon lemon juice

Instructions:
1. In frypan melt butter, add curry powder, celery, onion and pepper. Cook gently; stirring 2-3min.
2. Add tomato to pan and cook a further 2min.
3. Stir in flour, pepper and salt and cook, stirring for one minute.
4. Remove from heat; and gradually add water and milk. Add stock powder and return to heat. Cook, stirring, until sauce boils and thickens.
5. Transfer sauce to ovenproof shallow dish (the dish that comes with the extender kit is perfect)
6. Bake in NuWave oven; on 10cm rack for 10mins.
7. Add prawns; stir and bake a further 10mins.
8. Serve with plenty of steamed rice and enjoy!

Note:
Try pre-cooking your rice and using an ovenproof container (foil over the top) and place it on the liner tray to heat through/keep hot while the curry cooks!

139. Delicious Potato Topped Tilapia Fillets with A Herbed Sour Cream

Ingredients:
- 2 tilapia filets
- 1/2 egg
- 1 medium utility potato; peeled & rinsed in water
- 1 tablespoon cornstarch
- Pepper; to taste
- Salt; to taste
- 1/2 cup sour cream
- 1/2 lime; juiced
- 1 bunch fresh dill; finely minced

Instructions:
1. Thinly shred the potato and dry on a towel. Press tightly to squeeze the excess water out of the potatoes.
2. Place the dried-out potatoes in a small mixing bowl. Add in the cornstarch, beaten egg, salt and pepper. Mix well.
3. Spoon the prepared potato mixture over the tilapia fillets and lightly press.
4. Grease an ovenproof baking dish with some butter or spray with some cooking spray.
5. Place the potato topped tilapia fillets in the greased baking dish. Lightly pour some olive oil over them or spray with some cooking spray.
6. Place the baking dish on a 1-inch rack and cook on the 'HI' setting for about 18 to 20 minutes.
7. While the fish cooks; prepare the dipping sauce.
8. Place the sour cream in a small mixing bowl.
9. Add in dill, salt, lime juice and pepper. Mix well until all the ingredients are well incorporated.
10. When the fish is done remove the fillets from the oven on to a serving plate.
11. Serve hot; topped with a spoonful of the herbed sour cream.

140. Mouthwatering Moroccan Fish Skewers

Ingredients
- 8 pre-soaked bamboo skewers

Moroccan Spice Rub
- 2 teaspoon lemon pepper
- 1 teaspoon paprika
- 21 oz. (600g) ling fillets; cubed
- 1/2 teaspoon ground turmeric
- 1/2 teaspoon ground coriander

Instructions:

Make Moroccan spice rub:
1. Combine lemon pepper, paprika, turmeric and coriander in a glass or ceramic bowl.
2. Add fish, toss to coat. Cover. Refrigerate for 1 or 2 hours; if time permits.
3. Thread fish onto skewers.
4. Bake in NuWave oven on 10cm rack; power level HI, for 6-8 minutes or just cooked through (do not overcook).

141. Perfect Salmon Pie

Ingredients:
- 10.5 oz. (300g) fresh skinless salmon portions
- 1 tablespoon olive oil
- 1/2 med onion; finely chopped
- 1.7 oz. (50g) small mushrooms; finely slices
- 1/4 cup long grain cooked rice; cooled
- 1 teaspoon fresh dill; chopped
- 1 tablespoon thin cream
- 2 hardboiled eggs; chopped
- 2 sheets frozen puff pastry; thawed
- 1 extra egg; beaten

Instructions:
1. Wrap salmon in baking paper and bake in NuWave oven for 10-15 min (depending on thickness), on 10cm rack. Unwrap and allow to cool.
2. Heat oil in frypan; cook onions on med heat for 5mins; until soft.
3. Add mushrooms and cook further 2mins; until soft.
4. Transfer mixture to large mixing bowl and cool slightly.
5. Add rice, dill, cream and eggs, season with salt & pepper, mix well.
6. Lay out 1 sheet of pastry on baking paper and spread rice mixture down centre of pastry allowing 5cm at each end and 10cm either side.
7. Break salmon into chunks and place on top of rice.
8. Top with other sheet of pastry and gently mould it around the filling.
9. Cut sides to even them and fold all edges over toward center, pressing to seal.
10. Gently cut diagonal slits in top pastry and brush with extra egg.
11. Cook bottom side up, in NuWave oven on 5cm rack; for 10mins. Turn and cook a further 20 minutes.

142. Tasty Tuna and Sweetcorn Potatoes

Ingredients:
- 4 large potatoes (1.5kg)
- 0.8 oz. (25g) butter
- 1 onion; finely chopped
- 1 clove garlic
- 6.5 oz. (185g) can tuna; drained
- 11 oz. (310g) can sweet corn kernels; drained
- 1/3 cup sour cream
- 1/4 cup chopped fresh chives
- 1 cup grated tasty cheese
- salt & pepper; to taste

Instructions:
1. Wash unpeeled potatoes well and pierce all over with a fork. Cook in NuWave oven for 40 minutes or until tender.
2. Melt butter in frypan; add onion and garlic. Cook, stirring, for 2 minutes.
3. Cut potatoes in half (lengthways) and carefully scoop out flesh, leaving a 1cm thick shell. Place flesh in large bowl and mash with a fork.
4. Add tuna mixture, sour cream, chives and 1/2 cup of the cheese. Season with salt & pepper. Mix well.
5. Spoon filling back into potato half shells and sprinkle with remaining cheese.
6. Bake in NuWave oven on 5cm rack; level 10 for 15 minutes or until cheese has melted and golden brown. Serve with crisp garden salad.

143. Amazing Parmesan Topped Scallops

Ingredients:
- 8 sea scallops
- 2 teaspoon lime juice
- 2 tablespoon butter
- ½-cup grated parmesan cheese

Instructions:
1. Extract the muscle on the side of the sea scallops. Wash the scallops well and pat them dry using a kitchen towel.
2. Divide the scallops in 2 separate oven safe ramekins or in 2 real scallop shells. (You can find these at party supply stores)
3. Place about 1 tablespoon of butter over the scallops in the ramekins or in the shells.
4. Divide the lime juice and pour it over the butter.
5. Spoon the Parmesan cheese over the lime juice in two equal portions.
6. Place the ramekins on the 4-inch cooking rack.
7. Bake for about 8 to 10 minutes on the HI power setting or until the cheese on top is well browned.
8. Serve the scallops in the ramekin immediately.

144. Simple Tuna Steaks with a Tangy Orange Salsa

Ingredients for the Tuna:
- 2 (5–6-ounce) tuna steaks; 1/2-inch thick
- 1/2 tablespoon olive oil
- 1/4 teaspoon ground cumin
- 1/4 teaspoon black pepper
- 1/4 teaspoon salt

Ingredients for the Salsa:
- 1/2 teaspoon orange peel; finely shredded
- 1/2 large tomato; seeded and chopped
- 2 medium oranges; peeled, sectioned, and coarsely chopped
- 2 tablespoons fresh cilantro; snipped
- 1 tablespoon walnuts; chopped and toasted
- 1 tablespoon green onion; chopped
- 1/2 tablespoon lime juice
- 1/4 teaspoon black pepper
- 1/4 teaspoon salt

Instructions:
1. Place the cumin, pepper and salt together in a small mixing bowl. Mix well to combine.
2. Use a pastry brush to lightly oil the fish fillets and sprinkle the prepared cumin mixture onto the fillets.
3. Place the spiced fish fillets on a 3-inch rack.
4. Cook on the 'HI' setting for about 5 to 7 minutes per side or until the fish flakes easily when forked.
5. While the fish is cooking; prepare the orange salsa.
6. Place the tomato, coarsely chopped oranges, fresh cilantro, orange peel, walnuts and green onion together in a bowl. Mix well to combine.
7. Season the salsa with salt and pepper.
8. Pour the lemon juice over the salsa and let it sit for about 3 to 4 minutes.
9. Toss well until the salsa is well coated with the lemon juice.
10. Once the fish is done; transfer it to a serving plate and serve hot, topped with the prepared orange salsa.

145. Zesty Salmon With Fennel and Lemon

Ingredients:
- 1 (6 ounce) salmon filets; skin on
- 1 lemon; remove the zest and juice on ½ and cut the remaining ½ in slices
- ½ fennel bulb
- 1 tablespoon extra-virgin olive oil; divided
- Freshly ground black pepper; to taste
- Kosher salt; to taste

Instructions:
1. Tear two pieces of foil; each piece of foil should be bigger than the filet of the fish.
2. Rub a little oil on the foil and keep it aside.
3. Cut the fennel bulb into 4 equal pieces and remove its core. Slice it thinly.

4. Transfer the fennel slices to a medium bowl. Add in the lemon juice, salt, lemon zest, olive oil and pepper.
5. Toss until well coated and keep aside for about 10 minutes to marinate.
6. Divide the prepared fennel mixture into two equal parts and spoon onto the greased foil.
7. Use a kitchen towel to pat the fish filet dry and season using salt and pepper.
8. Place the seasoned salmon filet on the fennel mixture, with its skin side up.
9. Place about 2 lemon slices on each fish filet.
10. Fold the foil over the fish to create a loose packet and fold the ends to seal the packet.
11. Place the prepared fish packets on the 1-inch cooking rack and cook on the HI power setting for about 25 minutes or until the internal temperature of the fish reaches 145 degrees. And Serve hot.

146. Thai Style Chili Snapper

Ingredients:
- 1 snapper; whole with head removed (around 800g)
- 4 cloves garlic; crushed
- 1/4 cup finely chopped fresh lemongrass
- 1/4 cup chopped fresh coriander
- 2 fresh small red Thai chillies; chopped finely
- 2 tablespoons mild sweet chilli sauce
- 4cm piece fresh ginger; finely grated
- 1 tablespoon Thai red curry paste
- 2 tablespoon lime juice

Instructions:
1. Combine all ingredients except fish in a medium bowl.
2. Cut four shallow slits in each side of fish, making sure you don't cut through bones.
3. Coat both sides of fish with chilli mix and allow to marinate in fridge for 3 hours or overnight.
4. Pulling flaps of fish out; stand fish upright on 5cm rack.
5. Bake in NuWave oven for 20-25mins.

147. Tuna and Noodle Casserole

Ingredients:
- 5 tablespoon butter; divided
- 3 scallions; finely chopped and divided
- 1 ¼-cups flat egg noodles
- 1 ½ tablespoon flour
- 1 3/4 cups milk
- ½ teaspoon Dijon mustard
- Salt; to taste
- ½ can tuna; drained and broken into small chunks
- Freshly ground black pepper; to taste
- ¼-cup frozen peas
- Extra virgin olive oil; to taste
- 3/8 cup bread crumbs

Instructions:
1. Fill a 2-quart pot with water and heat over a high flame until the water is boiling.
2. Once the water is bubbling; add the noodles to the boiling water and cook for about 6 to 8 minutes.

3. Use a stainless steel steamer basket to drain the noodles.
4. Spoon the cooked noodles on a sheet pan and spread into an even layer. Pour the extra virgin olive oil over the noodles and keep aside.
5. Place about 2 tablespoon of butter in a medium sized frying pan and heat over a medium high flame.
6. Once the butter has melted; add about ½ the scallions to it and cook for about 2 to 3 minutes or until the scallions have softened.
7. Add the mustard and flour to the pan and cook for about 2 minutes while constantly stirring.
8. Slowly add in the milk, while whisking constantly to ensure there are no lumps.
9. Continue heating until the milk starts bubbling.
10. Keep cooking the sauce for another 18 to 20 minutes or until the sauce thickens and coats the back of the spoon.
11. Taste and season the sauce using salt and pepper.
12. Pour the sauce into a large bowl.
13. Add in the tuna, noodles and peas. Mix well until all the ingredients are well coated by the sauce.
14. Pour the prepared mixture into a 7.5-inch by 4.5 inch by 3-inch loaf pan. Keep aside.
15. Place the remaining butter in a small frying pan and heat over a medium flame.
16. Once the butter has melted; add in the remaining scallions. Cook the scallions until soft.
17. Add the breadcrumbs to the pan and continue mixing.
18. Cook for about 1 to 2 minutes or until the breadcrumbs are well browned.
19. Pour the prepared breadcrumb mix over the tuna mix.
20. Place the prepared loaf pan on the liner pan and bake for about 18 to 20 minutes on the 7-power setting. And Serve hot.

148. Hot & Zingy Clams & Sausage

Ingredients:
- 2 sausages; crumbled
- 2 cloves garlic; minced
- 16 littleneck clams; cleaned
- Chopped cilantro; to taste
- Hot sauce; to taste
- Lemon slices as needed

Instructions:
1. Place the sausage and clams together in a large mixing bowl.
2. Add in the cilantro, garlic and hot sauce to the bowl.
3. Toss until all the ingredients are well coated.
4. Arrange the clam and sausage mix in the bottom of the liner pan.
5. Cook on the 'HI' setting for about 12 to 15 minutes or until the sausage is cooked and the mussels open up.
6. Serve hot; topped with lemon slices.

149. Healthy Asparagus and Pesto Topped Orange Roughy

Ingredients:
- 1/3 cup readymade pesto
- 1/8 teaspoon hot sauce
- 1 tablespoon fresh lemon juice
- 2 (6 ounce) orange roughy filets
- ½ pint cherry tomatoes; sliced
- 8 asparagus spears; trimmed to 4-inches
- 1 yellow crookneck squash; thinly sliced

Instructions:
1. Place the pesto, hot sauce and lemon juice together in a small mixing bowl. Whisk using a wire whisk until the ingredients have emulsified.
2. Cut 2 12" x 12" pieces of heavy-duty aluminum foil and place them on a clean, dry and flat work surface.
3. Place 1 filet of the orange roughy in the center of the foil.
4. Sprinkle the pieces of fish with some salt and pepper.
5. Divide the pesto in four equal halves and spoon each quarter of the pesto over the seasoned fish filets.
6. Spread a layer of asparagus, squash and tomatoes on the layer of pesto.
7. Top with the remaining pesto.
8. Fold the foil over the fish and seal the packet of the fish.
9. Use a flat spatula to transfer the fish packets onto the 4-inch cooking rack.
10. Bake the fish on the HI power setting for about 12 to 14 minutes or until the fish can be easily forked.
11. Carefully open the foil packet and remove the fish from it. And Serve hot.

150. NuWave Style Quick N Easy Lobster Thermidor

Ingredients:
- 2 (4-6 ounce) lobster tail; shell removed and cut into 1-inch pieces
- 4 tablespoons heavy cream
- 4 tablespoons butter
- 4 tablespoons shallot; minced
- Chopped parsley
- 1 teaspoon dry mustard

Instructions:
1. Place the lobster tailpieces in an ovenproof dish.
2. Pour the heavy cream and butter over the pieces and mix well.
3. Add in the shallots and parsley and mix lightly until well coated.
4. Sprinkle the dry mustard on the top and mix again.
5. Place the baking dish on the 3-inch rack.
6. Cook on the 'HI' setting for about 12 to 15 minutes.
7. Remove the lobster pieces from the sauce and place on the serving plate.
8. Spoon the remaining sauce on the side.
9. Serve hot.

151. Cheesy Crab Dip with Toasted Wonton Wrappers

Ingredients:

- 1/2 (12-ounce) package 2-inch wonton wrappers; halved diagonally
- 4 ounces cream cheese; brought to room temperature
- Olive oil; to taste
- 2 tablespoons mayonnaise
- 6 ounces lump crab meat
- 2 tablespoons sour cream
- 1/2 cup shredded Cheddar cheese; divided
- 2 green onions; thinly sliced
- 2 tablespoons freshly grated Parmesan cheese
- 1/2 teaspoon Worcestershire sauce
- 1/2 teaspoon sesame oil
- 1/2 teaspoon soy sauce
- 1/4 teaspoon Sriracha (optional)
- Kosher salt; to taste
- 1/4 teaspoon garlic powder
- Freshly ground black pepper; to taste

Instructions:

1. Place the wonton wrapper halves in a flat plate. Drizzle the olive oil over them and toss well until well coated.
2. Spread the oil coated wonton wrappers in a single layer on a 3-inch rack.
3. Cook on the 'HI' setting for about 3 to 5 minutes on each side. Take care that the wonton wrappers do not burn.
4. Remove the toasted wanton wrappers from the oven and transfer them to a serving bowl to keep them warm.
5. Spray an ovenproof 10-inch baking dish with some cooking spray.
6. Place the cream cheese, sour cream and mayonnaise together in a large mixing bowl.
7. Whisk well until well combined.
8. Add in the crab meat, 1/4 cup Cheddar cheese, green onions, soy sauce, Sriracha, Parmesan, Worcestershire sauce, garlic powder and sesame oil. Mix well.
9. Season to taste with salt and pepper and mix well.
10. Transfer the prepared crabmeat mixture to the prepared baking dish and top with the remaining Cheddar cheese.
11. Place the baking dish on a 3-inch rack.
12. Cook on the 'HI' setting for about 15 to 17 minutes or until the cheese melts and lightly browns.
13. Serve hot with the warm toasted wonton wrappers.

152. Grilled Halibut with a Tangy Clementine Gremolata

Ingredients:

- 6 Clementines
- 4 garlic cloves; peeled and minced
- 2/3 cup chopped fresh Italian parsley
- 2 teaspoons sea salt
- 8 (6-ounce) halibut filets
- 1/2 cup extra-virgin olive oil
- Black pepper; to taste

Instructions:
1. Remove the peels of the clementines and place the flesh of the fruit in a small bowl.
2. Add in the sea salt, garlic and parsley and mix well until combined.
3. Add in the olive oil and let it stand for about 5 minutes.
4. Mix well and cover the bowl with a plastic wrap. Refrigerate for about an hour or until you need to use the Gremolata.
5. Rub the salt and pepper over the halibut filets and place the halibut fillets on a 1-inch rack.
6. Cook on the 'HI' setting for about 15 to 17 minutes. Flip the halibut fillets over around the 8-minute mark.
7. Check if the fish is done by flaking it with a fork.
8. If done; transfer the halibut fillets to a serving plate and serve hot topped with the chilled clementine Gremolata.

153. Oven Grilled Salmon

Ingredients:
- 2 (6 ounce) salmon fillets
- Salt; to taste
- 1 teaspoon chili powder
- 1 tablespoon olive oil
- Freshly ground black pepper; to taste

Instructions:
1. Combine the chili powder, pepper, salt and olive oil together in a small mixing bowl to prepare a spice rub.
2. Use your fingers to rub the prepared spice rub on the salmon filets.
3. Add the Extender Ring to the base if required.
4. Arrange the spice rub coated salmon filets on the 4-inch cooking rack in a single layer.
5. Grill on the HI power setting for about 8 to 10 minutes per side or until the fish breaks easily when forked.
6. Serve hot with the condiment of your choice.

154. Oven Fried Catfish

Ingredients:
- 1 cup yellow cornmeal
- 1 teaspoon salt
- 2 tablespoon flour
- ¼-teaspoon black pepper
- 1 egg
- 1/8 teaspoon cayenne pepper
- ½ pound catfish; cut into filets

Instructions:
1. Place the cornmeal, salt, cayenne pepper, flour and pepper together in a mixing bowl. Mix well until all the ingredients are completely combined. Keep aside.
2. Crack open the egg in another bowl and whisk using a wire whisk until lightly frothy.
3. Dip the catfish filets in the egg and turn them over until the filets are well coated in egg.
4. Place the egg coated fish filets in the cornmeal mix and toss until completely coated.

5. Place the flour covered catfish filets on the 1-inch cooking rack and cook at 420 degrees Fahrenheit for about 25 minutes or until the crust turns golden brown.
6. Serve hot with a fresh salad and your favorite condiment on the side.

155. Special Oven Grilled Tuna Steaks

Ingredients:
- 4 (6 – 8 ounce) tuna steaks
- 2 green bell peppers; deseeded and large diced
- 2 large onion; cut into large chunks
- 2 yellow bell peppers; deseeded and large diced
- 4 garlic cloves; minced
- 2 red bell peppers; deseeded and large diced
- 6 tablespoon fresh rosemary; chopped
- Freshly ground black pepper; to taste
- Kosher salt; to taste

Optional Ingredients:
- 1 lemon; squeezed for juice
- 4 tablespoon parmesan cheese; grated

Instructions:
1. Add the onions, salt, rosemary, lemon juice, green bell pepper, red bell pepper, yellow bell pepper, pepper, cheese and garlic to a large bowl. Mix well.
2. Wrap the 1-inch cooking wrap with some heavy-duty aluminum foil and spray some cooking spray over it.
3. Transfer the pepper and onion mixture onto the greased and foil covered rack.
4. Cook for about 13 to 15 minutes on the HI power setting.
5. Use a kitchen towel to pat dry the tuna steaks. Sprinkle pepper and salt on both sides of the tuna steaks.
6. Once the peppers and onions are done; place the seasoned tuna steaks over the cooked peppers and onions.
7. Cook for about 10 to 12 minutes on the HI power setting for medium done steaks, and bake for about 14 to 16 minutes for well-done steaks.
8. Transfer the tuna steaks onto serving plates and serve hot with a side of roasted peppers and onions.

156. Fennel Coated Bass

Ingredients:
- 12 ounces stripped or black bass; about 1-inch thick
- 2 tablespoons olive oil
- 2 teaspoons fennel seeds; crushed
- 2 tablespoons lemon juice
- Pepper; to taste
- Salt; to taste

Instructions:
1. In a small mixing bowl; combine together the olive oil, salt, fennel, lemon juice and pepper together. Mix well until well combined.
2. Divide the black or stripped bass fillet into two equal portions.

3. Place the bass fillets on a 3-inch rack and spoon the prepared fennel mixture onto the bass fillets.
   4. Cook on the 'HI' setting for about 10 to 12 minutes or until the fish easily flakes when struck with a fork.
   5. Serve hot with a salad of your choice on the side.

157. Spicy Red Snapper with Red Onion and Orange

Ingredients:
- 2 red snapper filets
- 1 teaspoon garlic; minced
- 2 tablespoons olive oil
- 1/2 tablespoon dark chili powder
- 1/2 red onion; small, sliced thin
- 1/2 orange; sliced
- 4 sprigs thyme
- 1 teaspoon black pepper
- 1/2 tablespoon kosher salt

Instructions:
1. Combine the olive oil, chili powder, pepper, garlic and salt together in a bowl. Mix well to forma smooth paste. Keep aside.
2. Place the snapper fillets on a cutting board with the skin side down. Spoon the prepared paste on the flesh side of each fillet and lightly rub it in.
3. Place the orange slices in the bottom of an airtight container in a single layer.
4. Top with a layer of red onion slices.
5. Sprinkle the thyme over it.
6. Place the red snapper fillets and seal the container.
7. Refrigerate for about 2 to 3 hours.
8. Place the red snapper fillets in a single layer on the 3-inch rack.
9. Top with a layer of red onions and orange slices (about 2 of each on each red snapper fillet).
10. Cook on the 'HI' setting for about 6 to 8 minutes on each side.
11. Remove the red snapper fillets from the oven and place on a serving plate.
12. Serve hot; topped with the grilled red onion and orange slices.

158. Tasty Oven Grilled Shrimp In Chipotle Sauce

Ingredients:
- 1-pound shrimp; cleaned and deveined (about 11 to 12 pieces)
- 1 ½ tablespoon chopped garlic
- ½ (15 ounce) chopped can tomatoes
- ½ small can chipotle sauce (whole chipotles blended into sauce)
- ½-cup cold water
- ½ small red onion; sliced

Instructions:
1. Place the shrimp in the liner pan.
2. Top the shrimp with the garlic and tomatoes and mix well.
3. Add in the chipotle sauce and cold water. Mix well.
4. Top with the red onion.

5. Cook on the HI power setting for about 12 to 14 minutes.
6. Serve hot with the condiment of your choice.

159. Baked Shrimp

Ingredients:
- 12 large shrimp; frozen, peeled and deveined
- 1/8 teaspoon ground cumin
- 1 tablespoon dark chili powder
- 1/8 teaspoon ground ginger

Instructions:
1. Combine the cumin, chili powder and ground ginger together in a small mixing bowl.
2. Transfer the spice mix to a salt shaker and keep aside.
3. Arrange the shrimp in a single layer on the 4-inch cooking rack.
4. Cook the shrimp for about 2 to 3 minutes on the HI power setting.
5. Carefully open the dome and sprinkle the seasoning on the shrimp.
6. Continue cooking the shrimp for another 6 to 7 minutes or until the shrimp become pink.
7. Serve hot with your favorite condiment on the size.

160. Tasty Tuna Noodle Casserole

Ingredients:
- 1 (5-ounce) can tuna; drained
- 1/2 (101/2-ounce) can cream of mushroom soup
- 1 cup egg noodles; cooked
- 1/4 cup water
- 1/4 cup sour cream
- 1/2 cup frozen peas or green beans; thawed
- 2 tablespoons breadcrumbs
- 1/2 cup Cheddar cheese; shredded and divided

Instructions:
1. Place the tuna, sour cream, green beans or peas, about 6 tablespoons cheese, cream of mushroom soup, and cooked noodles together in a medium mixing bowl.
2. Mix well until it forms a cohesive mixture.
3. Pour the prepared mix into an 8-inch ovenproof dish.
4. Place the ovenproof dish on the 1-inch rack and cook on the 'HI' setting for about 18 to 22 minutes.
5. Once the timer is up; add the remaining cheese and breadcrumbs on the top of the semi set casserole.
6. Bake on the 'HI' setting for another 2 to 3 minutes or until the cheese melts and gets light brown.
7. Once done; remove the casserole from the oven and cool for about 7 to 10 minutes before serving.
8. Serve hot.

VEGETARIAN RECIPES

Ingredients:
- 12 large closed cup mushrooms
- 1/4 cup ricotta cheese
- 1/2 cup fresh spinach
- 2 tablespoon parmesan cheese; grated
- 1 garlic clove
- 1/2 small onion
- 2 tablespoon vegetable stock

Instructions:
1. Pop the stems out of the mushrooms and wipe them clean
2. Place all the remaining ingredients in the short cup of NuWave Twister and fit the cross blade. Pulse until almost smooth. Spoon mixture into the mushrooms.
3. Bake in NuWave oven on 10cm rack; level 10 for 15mins.

161. Cheesy Zucchini and Onion Au Gratin

Ingredients:
- 1/2 large yellow onion; cut into 1/2-inch pieces
- 1/2 tablespoon olive oil
- 1/2 medium zucchini; cut into 1/2-inch slices
- 1/4 cup Cheddar cheese; shredded
- Pepper; to taste
- Salt; to taste

Instructions:
1. Place the yellow onion in a single layer in the liner pan and pour in the olive oil. Toss well.
2. Cook on the 'HI' setting for about 13 to 15 minutes. Around the 8-minute mark; toss the onions around.
3. Place the zucchini slices in a single layer over the grilled onions.
4. Sprinkle salt and pepper to taste.
5. Return the liner pan to the oven and cook on the 'HI' setting for another 5 to 7 minutes.
6. Sprinkle the cheese over the zucchini and cook for an extra 2 to 3 minutes or until the cheese melts.
7. Serve hot.

162. Creamy Baked Sweet Potatoes

Ingredients:
- 1 tablespoon olive oil
- 1 tablespoon brown sugar
- 3 medium sweet potatoes (6 - 8 - oz. each)
- 1 tablespoon unsalted butter; melted
- 1 tablespoon cream

Instructions:
1. Pour the olive oil over the potatoes and rub it using your fingers.
2. Place the olive oil coated potatoes on the 3-inch cooking rack.

3. Bake the potatoes for about 35 to 40 minutes at 420 degrees Fahrenheit.
4. Once done; cool the potatoes until manageable.
5. Once manageable; slice the potatoes in half.
6. Scoop the flesh from two potatoes into a large mixing bowl, leaving about ½ inch of flesh attached to the skin.
7. Scoop out all the flesh from the last potato so that you have enough potato flesh in order to fill the remaining two potato skins.
8. Add the brown sugar; melted butter and brown sugar to the potato flesh. Mix well until the potato and sugar mixture is smooth.
9. Spoon the prepared mixture into the 4 potato halves and place the stuffed potatoes on the 3-inch cooking rack.
10. Bake for about 7 to 9 minutes at 400 degrees Fahrenheit. And Serve hot.

163. Herbed Winter Vegetables

Ingredients:
- ½ medium butternut squash; peeled and diced
- 1-pound baby potatoes; scrubbed and halved
- 1 medium red beet; scrubbed, peeled and diced
- 1 large onion; cut into 1-inch wedges
- Kosher salt; to taste
- ¼-cup olive oil
- Freshly ground black pepper; to taste
- 1 large parsnip; peeled and cut into 1-inch pieces
- ½ pound Brussels sprouts; trimmed and halved
- ½ tablespoon finely chopped rosemary
- ½ tablespoon paprika
- ½ tablespoon finely chopped thyme
- 1 tablespoon parsley

Instructions:
1. Place the butternut squash, baby potatoes, red beet, onion, parsnip and Brussels sprouts together in a large mixing bowl.
2. Add in the olive oil, kosher salt, black pepper, rosemary, paprika, thyme and parsley and toss well until well coated.
3. Transfer the olive oil and seasoning tossed vegetables to the liner pan.
4. Grill for about 30 to 40 minutes at about 400 degrees Fahrenheit. And Serve hot.

164. Delicious Feta and Artichoke Tortilla Wraps with a Chive and Yogurt Dip

Ingredients:
- 1/2 (14-ounce) can artichoke hearts; drained and chopped finely
- 2 green onions; thinly chopped
- 1/4 cup cream cheese
- 2/3 cup Parmesan or Romano cheese; grated
- 2 tablespoons pesto
- 2 tablespoons Feta cheese; crumbled
- 4 whole tortillas (8-inch)
- 1/2 (8-ounce) carton plain fat-free yogurt

- 1/2 (7-ounce) jar of sweet peppers; water drained and cut vertically
- 1/2 tablespoon chives; roughly chopped

Instructions:
1. Grease an 8-inches by 8-inch silicone baking dish with some butter or spray it with some cooking spray. Keep aside.
2. Place the artichoke hearts, green onions, Feta cheese, cream cheese, Parmesan cheese and pesto together in a large mixing bowl. Mix well until well combined.
3. Place about 2 tablespoons of this mix on each tortilla.
4. Top the cream cheese mixture with red pepper strips.
5. Roll the tortilla into a tight roll.
6. Place the tortilla rolls in the prepared silicon-baking dish. Spray lightly with some cooking spray.
7. Place the tortilla filled baking dish on a 3-inch cooking rack.
8. Cook on the 'HI' setting for about 12 to 15 minutes or until the tortillas are thoroughly heated.
9. While the tortilla rolls heat through, prepare the sipping sauce.
10. Combine the chives and yogurt together in a small mixing bowl. Keep aside.
11. Once cooked thoroughly, cut the rolls in 3 parts and place on a serving plate.
12. Serve hot with the chive and yogurt sauce on the side.

165. Crunchy French Beans with Almond Topped

Ingredients:
- 6 ounces French green beans; trimmed and rinsed
- 2 tablespoons lemon juice
- 1 tablespoon olive oil
- 1/4 cup almonds; sliced
- 1/2 cup crispy fried onion ringlets
- 1 tablespoon butter; melted

Instructions:
1. Place the French beans in an ovenproof 8-inches by 8-inches baking dish.
2. Pour the lemon juice and olive oil over the French beans and place the baking dish on the 1-inch rack.
3. Cook on the 'HI' setting for about 10 to 12 minutes.
4. Sprinkle the almonds and onions over the beans and continue cooking for another 4 to 5 minutes on the 'HI' setting.
5. Remove from the oven and serve immediately.

166. Spicy Grilled Vegetables with a Yogurt and Tahini Dip

Ingredients:
- 1/2 cup plain fat-free Greek-style yogurt
- 1/2 tablespoon fresh lemon juice
- 3/4 tablespoons tahini
- 1/4 teaspoon ground cumin
- 1/4 teaspoon salt; divided
- 1/2 teaspoon garlic; minced
- 2 tablespoons olive oil

- 6 large button mushrooms
- 1/4 teaspoon Spanish smoked paprika
- 1 tomato; halved horizontally
- 1/2 head of radicchio; quartered
- 1 (3/4 pound) eggplant; cut lengthwise into 4 wedges
- 1/2 medium onion; quartered
- Fresh parsley; chopped (optional)
- 1/4 teaspoon black pepper
- 2 Kaiser Rolls

Instructions:
1. Combine the yogurt, lemon juice, garlic, tahini, cumin and 1/4 teaspoon salt together in a mixing bowl. Whisk using a wire whisk until well combined. Cover with a plastic wrap and refrigerate.
2. In another bowl; pour the oil and add in the paprika. Whisk well until well combined.
3. Place the mushrooms, eggplant, onion, tomato and radicchio together in a bowl.
4. Pour the prepared paprika oil over the vegetables and toss well until well coated.
5. Spread the paprika oil coated vegetables on the 1-inch rack in a single layer.
6. Grill on the 'HI' setting for about 20 to 22 minutes.
7. Around the 10-minute mark, open the dome and mix the vegetables around a bit.
8. Spoon the grilled vegetables on to a serving plate and serve hot with a side of the prepared yogurt and tahini sauce and Kaiser rolls.

167. Streusel Topped Buttery Sweet Potato Casserole

Ingredients:
- 2 sweet potatoes
- 1/4 cup sugar
- 2/3 cup and 2 tablespoons butter
- 1/4 cup brown sugar
- 1/4 teaspoon salt
- 1 egg; slightly beaten
- 1/2 teaspoon vanilla
- 2 tablespoons pecans; chopped
- 6 teaspoons and 1 teaspoon flour

Instructions:
1. Lightly fork the sweet potatoes and place them on a 3-inch rack.
2. Cook on the 'HI' setting for about 40 to 45 minutes.
3. Remove the sweet potatoes from the oven and cool for about 15 to 20 minutes.
4. Once cool enough to handle; peel the sweet potatoes.
5. Place the sweet potatoes in a medium sized bowl and mash into a smooth pulp.
6. Add in the 2/3-cup butter, egg, vanilla, sugar, salt and 1 teaspoon flour. Mix well until all the ingredients are well incorporated.
7. Pour the mixture into a 1-quart ovenproof casserole dish.
8. Place the casserole dish on the 1-inch rack.
9. Cook on the 'HI' setting for about 22 to 25 minutes.
10. While the casserole bakes; combine the remaining flour, leftover butter, pecans and brown sugar together in a mixing bowl.
11. Mix well until combined.

12. Once the timer is up, remove the dome and stir the casserole.
13. Pour the prepared streusel mix over the casserole in an even layer.
14. Continue baking on the 'HI' setting for another 12 to 15 minutes.
15. Serve hot.

168. Classical Stuffed Capsicums

Ingredients:
- 2 green capsicums
- 1 tablespoon oil
- 1 oz. (30g) butter
- 1/2 small onion; finely chopped
- 1/4 cup celery; finely chopped
- 9 oz. (250g) minced meat
- 1/2 cup cooked rice
- 1/4 teaspoon chilli flakes
- 1/4 teaspoon paprika
- 1 teaspoon dried Italian herbs
- 1 tablespoon tomato salsa
- 1/4 cup parmesan cheese

Instructions:
1. Cut capsicums lengthways; remove seeds and membranes. Place capsicums in boiling water with oil and boil for 3 minutes. Drain well. Season inside of capsicums with salt and pepper.
2. Heat butter; add onion and celery, sauté until tender; add meat, rice, chilli, paprika and herbs.
3. Cook, stirring constantly; until meat changes colour. Stir in salsa.
4. Place meat mixture into capsicum halves and top with parmesan cheese.
5. Bake in NuWave oven on 5cm rack for 15-20mins (depending on size of capsicums).

169. Tofu, Cheese and Marinara Sauce Stuffed Bell Peppers

Ingredients:
- 1/2 cup brown rice
- 1 cup marinara sauce; divided
- 1/2 (12-ounce) tofu; drained and diced
- Salt; to taste
- 2 bell peppers; 1/4 tops cut off and seeds removed
- Pepper; to taste
- 4 (1/2-inch) slices tomato
- 1 cup Mozzarella cheese; shredded and divided

Instructions:
1. Follow the instructions on the package and cook the brown rice.
2. Place the peppers in a baking dish.
3. Spoon about 1/4 cup of brown rice into each bell pepper.
4. Spoon about 1/2 cup of the marinara sauce over the layer of the brown rice and top with about 1/4- cup mozzarella cheese each.
5. Divide the tofu equally between the two bell peppers and place over the layer of mozzarella cheese.
6. Place one slice of tomato on each bell pepper.
7. Sprinkle the remaining cheese over the bell peppers.

8. Cover the baking dish with a sheet of aluminum foil and bake on the 'HI' setting for about 18 to 20 minutes.
9. Remove the aluminum sheet and bake for another 3 to 4 minutes on the 'HI' setting.
10. Serve hot with a side of your favorite condiment.

170. Roasted Chickpeas, Cauliflower and Olives

Ingredients:
- 3 cups cauliflower florets
- 4 cloves garlic; coarsely chopped
- ½-cup Spanish green olives; pitted
- ½ (15 ounce) can garbanzo beans (chickpeas); rinsed and drained
- ¼-teaspoon crushed red pepper
- 1 ½ tablespoon olive oil
- 1 ½ tablespoon fresh flat leaf parsley
- 1/8 teaspoon salt

Instructions:
1. Place the cauliflower florets, garlic, Spanish green olives and garbanzo beans together in a large mixing bowl.
2. Add the red pepper, flat leaf parsley and salt and mix well.
3. Pour the olive oil into the bowl and toss well to coat.
4. Empty the bowl into the liner pan and spread it into an even layer.
5. Grill the veggies for about 17 to 20 minutes at 400 degrees Fahrenheit or on the HI power setting or until the vegetables are tender and browned. And Serve hot.

171. Delicious Ricotta and Spinach Stuffer Lasagna Rolls

Ingredients:
- 4 lasagna noodles; cooked and drained
- 1 clove garlic; minced
- 1/2 medium onion; finely chopped
- 1/2 tablespoon butter
- 1/2 teaspoon oregano
- 1 1/2 cups tomato sauce
- 1/4 teaspoon thyme leaves
- 2 tablespoons mushrooms; chopped (optional)
- 1/4 teaspoon basil
- 1 (5 ounce) package frozen chopped spinach
- 1 tablespoon Parmesan cheese
- 1/2 cup Ricotta or cottage cheese
- Dash black pepper

Instructions:
1. Follow the instructions on the package and cook the noodles according to the instructions.
2. Heat the butter in a saucepan and add in the garlic and onion.
3. Sauté for a few minutes until the onion turns translucent and the garlic is aromatic.
4. Pour in the tomato sauce and mix well.
5. Add in the oregano, thyme leave and basil. Mix well and cook for 1 minute.
6. Add in the mushrooms and let the sauce simmer for about 8 to 10 minutes or until the sauce starts to bubble.
7. Take the sauce off the heat and keep it aside.

8. Follow the instructions on the package and cook the spinach. Drain the water from the spinach and squeeze until all the excess water is drained.
9. Place the spinach, pepper, Ricotta (or cottage cheese) and Parmesan cheese together in the jar of a blender. Blitz until smooth.
10. Spoon the mixture onto the end of a lasagna noodle.
11. Roll the noodle tightly to contain the filling in.
12. Repeat with the rest of the lasagna noodles.
13. Place the lasagna noodle rolls in a liner pan that has been sprayed with cooking spray.
14. Pour the prepared sauce over the lasagna noodle rolls.
15. Cook on the 'HI' setting for about 20 to 25 minutes or until the noodle rolls are heated through.
16. Serve hot.

172. Roasted Cauliflower, Olives and Chickpeas

Ingredients:
- 3 cups cauliflower florets
- 4 cloves garlic; coarsely chopped
- 1/2 cup Spanish green olives; pitted
- 1/2 (15-ounce) can chickpeas; rinsed and drained
- 1/4 teaspoon crushed red pepper
- 1 1/2 tablespoons olive oil
- 1 1/2 tablespoons fresh flat leaf parsley
- 1/4 teaspoon salt

Instructions:
1. Place the cauliflower florets, garlic, Spanish green olives, chickpeas, crushed red pepper, parsley and salt together in a large mixing bowl.
2. Pour the olive oil over the ingredients and let it stand for about 2 to 3 minutes.
3. Toss until all the ingredients are well coated in the olive oil.
4. Place the olive oil coated ingredients in the bottom of a liner pan in a single even layer.
5. Cook on the 'HI' setting for about 22 to 24 minutes.
6. Serve hot with your preferred condiment on the side.

173. Parmesan Crusted Asparagus Spears with Balsamic Vinegar

Ingredients:
- 1/2-pound asparagus
- 1/2-ounce Parmesan cheese; shaved
- 1/2 tablespoon extra-virgin olive oil
- 2 tablespoons balsamic vinegar
- Black pepper; to taste

Instructions:
1. Rinse the asparagus well and trim its ends.
2. Pour the olive oil over the asparagus spears and toss well until well coated.
3. Spread the oil coated asparagus on the 3-inch rack in a single layer.
4. Sprinkle the cheese over the asparagus and cook on the 'HI' setting for about 8 to 10 minutes.
5. Remove the Parmesan crusted asparagus spears on to a serving plate.

6. Pour the balsamic vinegar over the asparagus.
7. Serve immediately.

174. Roasted Mushrooms

Ingredients:
- 1 (8 ounce) package button mushrooms or crimini; cut into quarters
- 2 cloves garlic; finely chopped
- 1 ½ tablespoon olive oil
- 2 tablespoon fresh thyme; chopped
- Freshly ground black pepper; to taste
- Salt; to taste

Instructions:
1. Place the olive oil, garlic, thyme, salt and black pepper together. Whisk well until well combined.
2. Place the mushrooms in a large mixing bowl and pour the prepared marinade over it.
3. Toss well until the mushrooms are well coated.
4. Place the mushroom in a single layer into the liner pan.
5. Grill the mushrooms for about 20 to 22 minutes at 350 degrees Fahrenheit. And Serve hot.

175. Delicious Mayonnaise & Cheese Covered Corn

Ingredients:
- 4 ears of corn; cut into about 4 pieces each
- 1/2 cup mayonnaise
- 1/2 cup melted butter
- 1 cup Queso or Cotija cheese
- Chili powder or paprika; to taste
- Fresco; grated
- Salt; to taste
- 16 lime wedges (optional)
- Pepper; to taste

Instructions:
1. Place the corncob pieces on the 3-inch rack.
2. Grill on the 'HI' setting for about 8 to 10 minutes on each side.
3. Remove the corncobs from the oven and immediately pour the butter on each piece of corn.
4. Pour the mayonnaise on the corn.
5. Sprinkle the cheese, salt, chili powder and pepper over the mayonnaise covered corn pieces.
6. Serve hot with lime wedges on the side.

176. Roasted Garlic Mushrooms

Ingredients:
- 1 (8-ounce) package crimini or button mushrooms; quartered
- 2 cloves garlic; finely chopped
- 2 tablespoon olive oil
- 1 tablespoon fresh thyme; chopped
- Freshly ground black pepper; to taste
- Salt; to taste

Instructions:

1. Place the olive oil; garlic and fresh thyme together in a small mixing bowl. Whisk well until well combined.
2. Season to taste with salt and pepper.
3. Pour the marinade over the mushrooms and toss well until the mushrooms are well coated.
4. Place the marinated mushrooms directly onto the liner pan.
5. Roast on the 'HI' setting for about 20 to 25 minutes.
6. Serve hot.

177. Spicy Roasted Corn and Zucchini

Ingredients:
- ½ pound medium zucchini; cut lengthwise, further cut cross wise into 3-inch spears
- 1 (16-ounce) packages frozen corn
- 1 garlic clove; minced
- Salt; to taste
- 1 teaspoon chili powder
- 1 tablespoon olive oil
- Black pepper as per taste

Optional Ingredients:
- Lime wedges
- ¼-cup chopped scallions

Instructions:
1. Place the zucchini, garlic, olive oil, corn and chili powder together and mix well until well combined.
2. Season to taste with salt and pepper and toss again.
3. Transfer the vegetables to a silicone pizza liner or a cookie sheet.
4. Place the pizza liner or the cookie sheet on the 4-inch cooking rack and cook on the HI power setting for about 18 to 20 minutes or until the vegetables are tender and browned.
5. Serve hot topped with some scallions and lime wedges.

178. Chive Topped Potatoes

Ingredients:
- 1 medium russet potato; washed and cut into 1/8-inch slices
- Kosher salt; to taste
- 1 ½ tablespoon butter; melted
- Freshly ground black pepper; to taste

Optional Ingredients:
- Chives

Instructions:
1. Pour a little butter (about 1/2teaspoon) into the bottom of an 8-inch baking pan. Swirl the butter around to grease the bottom and sides of the baking pan.
2. Place the potato slices in the greased pan in a spiral pattern, starting from the outside and working towards the center.
3. Brush some butter onto the potatoes and sprinkle pepper and salt over the potatoes.
4. Repeat the steps 2 and 3 until all the potato slices have been arranged in the pan.

5. Place the prepared pan on the 1-inch cooking rack.
6. Cook on the HI power setting for about 35 to 40 minutes or until the potatoes are tender.
7. Remove the pan from the oven and sprinkle the chives over the potatoes.
8. Invert the potatoes on a serving plate and serve hot.

179. Ricotta and Spinach Stuffed Jumbo Pasta Shells

Ingredients:
- 6 jumbo pasta shells
- ¼-cup shredded parmesan cheese; divided (about 4 tablespoons)
- 1 cup ricotta cheese
- 5 - oz. spinach; sautéed
- Salt; to taste
- ½ egg; slightly beaten
- Freshly ground black pepper; to taste
- ½ (26-ounce) jar spaghetti sauce; divided
- ½ teaspoon Italian seasoning

Instructions:
1. Follow the instructions on the package of the jumbo shells and prepare the jumbo pasta shells. Drain from the water and keep them aside.
2. Place the ricotta cheese in a large mixing bowl. Add in about 2 tablespoon Parmesan, egg, pepper, spinach, salt and Italian seasoning.
3. Mix well until all the ingredients are well combined.
4. Spoon the prepared mixture into the cooked jumbo pasta shells.
5. Spread about 6 tablespoon of the spaghetti sauce in the bottom of a 4-inch by 4-inch baking pan.
6. Place the spinach and ricotta stuffed pasta shells in the baking pan.
7. Pour the remaining spaghetti sauce over the pasta shells and top with the remaining 2 tablespoon Parmesan cheese.
8. Place the baking pan on the 1-inch cooking rack and bake for about 15 to 17 minutes at 375 degrees Fahrenheit or until the cheese is bubbling and becomes brown around the edges. And Serve hot.

180. Crust less Quiche - Mushroom and Bacon

Ingredients:
- 6 rashers of rindless bacon; diced
- 1tablespoon oil
- 1 medium onion; finely diced
- 12.5 oz. (350g) button mushrooms; halved
- 6 eggs; lightly whisked
- 1/2 cup milk
- 2/3 cup sour cream
- 1 cup grated cheddar cheese
- 1 1/2 cups stale white coarse breadcrumbs (this will take about 2 slices of toast thick bread for food processor)
- 1.5 oz. (40g) butter; melted

Instructions:
1. Using the 23cm pan that comes with the NuWave oven extender kit; add bacon and cook on 10cm rack in NuWave oven for 8min until crisp.
2. Add onion and mushrooms to pan; stir well and cook a further 3mins.
3. Transfer mushroom mixture to base of greased 26cm pie dish.
4. In medium bowl whisk eggs, sour cream, milk and cheese; pour over bacon mixture.
5. Combine breadcrumbs and butter in a small bowl: sprinkle over egg mixture.
6. Cook on 5cm rack in NuWave oven for 30-40mins. Pie will puff up and pull slightly away from the sides when cooked.
7. Allow to stand for 10 minutes before serving.

181. Roasted Russet Potatoes

Ingredients:
- 3/4-pound russet potatoes; scrubbed well and cut into quarters
- ½ tablespoon fresh thyme; minced
- 2 tablespoon extra virgin olive oil
- ½ tablespoon oregano; minced
- Kosher salt; to taste
- ½ teaspoon fresh rosemary leaves; minced
- Freshly ground black pepper; to taste

Instructions:
1. Place the quartered potatoes in a large mixing bowl. Pour the olive oil over the potatoes and toss well until well coated.
2. Add the thyme, oregano, rosemary leaves, salt and pepper to the mixing bowl and toss well.
3. Place the herbed potatoes on the 4-inch cooking rack and bake on the HI power setting for about 10 to 12 minutes.
4. Flip the potatoes over and continue cooking for another 10 to 12 minutes. and Serve hot.

182. Baked Tomato and Cheese Casserole

Ingredients:
- 2 tablespoon olive oil; divided
- ½ (14-ounce) can whole plum tomatoes; peeled and drained
- ½-cup bread crumbs
- ½ (14-ounce) can diced tomatoes; drained
- 1 clove garlic; minced
- 1 tablespoon olive oil
- 4 mini fresh mozzarella balls; cut into quarters (¼-cup)
- ½ tablespoon melted butter
- 5 basil leaves; thinly sliced and divided
- Salt; to taste
- ½ tablespoon parmesan cheese; shredded
- Freshly ground black pepper; to taste

Instructions:
1. Place the breadcrumbs and 1-tablespoon olive oil together in a medium sized baking dish. Toss well until the breadcrumbs are slightly moistened. Keep aside.
2. Pour the remaining olive oil into a large mixing bowl.

3. Add in the whole plum tomatoes, diced tomatoes, garlic, mozzarella balls, butter, basil leaves, Parmesan cheese, salt and pepper and mix well until well combined.
4. Grease an 8-inch by 8-inch dish with the remaining olive oil.
5. Pour the prepared tomato and cheese mix into the greased baking dish.
6. Top the mixture with the prepared breadcrumb and olive oil mixture.
7. Place the baking dish on the 1-inch cooking rack.
8. Bake for about 15 to 20 minutes at 350 degrees Fahrenheit or until the top gets crisp. And Serve hot.

183. Herbed Fingerling Potatoes

Ingredients:
- 1 teaspoon coarse salt
- 1/8 teaspoon finely chopped fresh thyme
- 1/8 teaspoon freshly ground pepper
- 1/8 teaspoon finely chopped fresh rosemary
- ½ tablespoon extra-virgin olive oil
- 3/4 pounds fingerling potatoes; scrubbed

Instructions:
1. Combine the pepper, rosemary, salt and thyme together in a small mixing bowl. Keep aside.
2. Place the fingerling potatoes in a medium bowl and pour the olive oil over the potatoes. Toss well until well coated.
3. Sprinkle the seasoned salt over the oil coated potatoes. Toss the potatoes well until well coated.
4. Arrange the seasoned potatoes in a single and even layer on the 3-inch cooking rack.
5. Grill the potatoes at 350 degrees Fahrenheit for about 15 to 17 minutes or until the potatoes are grilled on the outside and softened on the inside. And Serve hot.

184. Vegetables Stuffed Mushrooms

Ingredients:
- 2 large field mushrooms
- 1 tablespoon oil
- 0.5 oz. (15g) butter
- 1/2 teaspoon plain flour
- 1/8 teaspoon French mustard
- 2 tablespoon milk
- 1 tablespoon tasty cheese; grated
- 1/2 cup frozen mixed vegetables
- 1/2 tablespoon flat leaf parsley; chopped
- grated tasty cheese; extra
- pepper & salt to taste

Instructions:
1. Remove centre core of mushrooms and discard. Rub outer side of mushrooms with the oil.
2. Make a thick cheese sauce by melting butter in a small saucepan, add flour and stir over heat for 1 minute.

3. Remove from heat and gradually add the milk and mustard. Return to heat and stir constantly until thick (feel free to add a touch more milk if necessary but remember that it is meant to be quite thick).
4. Stir in cheese until melted.
5. Add the mixed vegetables and parsley.
6. Fill mushrooms with the vegetable mixture and top with extra cheese
7. Bake in NuWave oven on 10cm rack for 8-10mins.

185. Quick and Easy Roasted Butternut Squash

Ingredients:
- 1/2 butternut squash; cut in half lengthwise and seeds removed
- 1 teaspoon salt
- 1 teaspoon sugar
- Extra-virgin olive oil; as needed

Instructions:
1. Prepare the squash as per the instructions and keep aside.
2. Pour the olive oil over the squash.
3. Combine the sugar and salt together and rub it over the butternut squash half.
4. Place the butternut squash half on a 1-inch rack.
5. Cook on the 'HI' setting for about 35 to 45 minutes.
6. Chop the roasted squash into cubes.
7. Transfer the roasted squash cubes onto a serving plate.
8. Serve hot, topped with some olive oil for garnish.

186. Pinto Bean Burgers

Ingredients:
- ½ tablespoon sunflower oil; plus extra for brushing
- ½ garlic clove; finely chopped
- ½ onion; finely chopped
- ½ teaspoon coriander
- 2 - oz. white mushrooms; finely chopped
- ½ teaspoon ground cumin
- ½ (15 ounce) can pinto or red kidney beans; drained and rinsed
- 2 slices provolone cheese
- 1 tablespoon fresh flat leaf parsley; chopped
- 2 ciabatta buns
- Salt; to taste
- All-purpose flour; for dusting
- Freshly ground black pepper; to taste

Instructions:
1. Place the pinto beans in a medium sized mixing bowl. Use a fork or the back of a spoon to mash the beans until smooth.
2. Add the mushrooms, onions, garlic, oil, coriander, cumin, and parsley. Mix well until all the ingredients are well combined.
3. Divide the bean mix into two equal portions and sprinkle a little flour on each half.

4. Shape the bean mix into a patty that is about 1-inch thick.
5. Brush some oil on the patties and place them on the 4-inch cooking rack.
6. Grill the patties on the HI power setting for about 5 to 8 minutes on each side.
7. Place the cheese on the patties and continue cooking for another 2 minutes or until the cheese is melted.
8. Slice the Ciabatta buns into halves and place the patties in them.
9. Serve hot with toppings and sides of your choice.

187. Easy Cheesy Quesadillas

Ingredients:
- 4 (10 inch) flour tortillas
- 4 tablespoon chopped cilantro
- 3 cups white Mexican cheese

Optional Ingredients:
- 3 cups sliced sweet bell pepper
- Sour cream
- Salsa to dip

Instructions:
1. Place two tortillas on the 4-inch cooking rack.
2. Sprinkle the cheese, sweet peppers and cilantro in equal amounts on both of the tortillas.
3. Top the tortillas with the remaining tortillas.
4. Secure the tortillas with toothpicks or place the 2-inch cooking rack over the quesadillas to ensure that the top tortilla doesn't fly off.
5. Cook on the HI power setting for about 4 to 5 minutes.
6. Flip the quesadilla over and continue cooking for another 3 to 4 minutes.
7. Transfer the quesadilla to the cutting board and slice it into 4 pieces.
8. Serve hot salsa or sour cream.

188. Cauliflower and Broccoli Gratin

Ingredients:
- ½-cup Italian-seasoned bread crumbs
- 8 - oz. fresh broccoli florets
- 8 - oz. fresh cauliflower florets
- 1 tablespoon olive oil
- 3/4 cup mayonnaise
- ½-cup shredded mozzarella cheese
- ½-cup shredded cheddar cheese
- 2 green onions; sliced
- 1/8 teaspoon cayenne
- 1 tablespoon Dijon mustard

Instructions:
1. Place the breadcrumbs in a medium sized dish. Pour the olive oil over the breadcrumbs and mix well until the breadcrumbs are lightly moist.
2. Arrange the broccoli florets and the cauliflower florets in the steamer basket.
3. Place the steamer basket over a pot of boiling water.
4. Cover the basket and steam for about 5 to 8 minutes or until the florets are tender. Drain the water from the florets until dry.

5. Grease a 1-quart baking dish with some butter or cooking spray.
6. Place the steamed broccoli florets and cauliflower in the prepared baking dish.
7. In a separate mixing bowl; combine together the mayonnaise, onions, cayenne, cheese and mustard together. Mix well until all the ingredients are well incorporated.
8. Spoon the prepared mix over the steamed florets.
9. Sprinkle some breadcrumbs over the florets and place the baking dish on the 1-inch cooking rack.
10. Bake for about 25 to 30 minutes at 350 degrees Fahrenheit. And Serve hot.

189. Butter Hassel back Potatoes

Ingredients:
- 2 garlic cloves; smashed
- Butter; as needed
- 6 tablespoon olive oil; divided
- Saffron; as needed
- 6 Idaho potatoes

Instructions:
1. Combine the garlic, butter and olive oil together in a small oven safe baking dish.
2. Place the baking dish on the 4-inch cooking rack and cook on the HI power setting for about 4 to 5 minutes.
3. Carefully extract the baking dish from the oven.
4. While the butter is melting in the oven, place the Idaho potatoes horizontally on a cutting board.
5. Starting on one end; slowly make thin slices, cutting about three quarters through the potatoes.
6. Place the potatoes on the 4-inch cooking rack and brush the prepared garlic butter over the potatoes.
7. Bake the potatoes on the HI power setting for about 60 to 70 minutes.
8. Serve hot with the condiment of your choice.

DESSERTS & PUDDINGS

190. Greek Style Lemon Yoghurt Syrup Cake

Ingredients:
- 8.8 oz. (250g) butter; softened
- 3 teaspoon lemon rind; finely grated
- 3/4 cup caster sugar
- 3 eggs
- 1 1/4 cups Greek-style yoghurt
- 1/4 cup lemon juice
- 1 1/2 cups self-raising flour
- 1/2 cup plain flour

Instructions:
1. Grease a fluted ring pan (or Bundt pan).
2. Using an electric mixer, beat butter, lemon rind and sugar until light and fluffy.
3. Add eggs, 1 at a time, beating well after each addition.
4. Transfer mixture to a large bowl, add half the yoghurt and half the lemon juice; stir to combine; sift half the flours over butter mixture; stir to combine. Repeat with remaining yoghurt, lemon juice and flours.
5. Spread mixture into prepared pan.
6. Bake on 5cm rack in NuWave oven; power level HI for 45 mins or until skewer inserted in cake comes out clean. Cool in pan for 10 mins. Turn out onto a wire rack over a baking tray.

Meanwhile; make lemon syrup:
1. Combine lemon juice, sugar and 1/4 cup cold water in a saucepan over low heat.
2. Stir for about 5 mins or until sugar has dissolved; increase heat to medium; bring to the boil, reduce heat to low and simmer for about 5 minutes or until thickened.
3. Pour hot syrup over hot cake.

191. Pumpkin Cookie Sandwiches with a Cream Cheese Filling

Ingredients:
- 1/2 cup vegetable oil
- 1 large egg
- 1 cup light brown sugar
- 1/2 cup pumpkin puree
- 1/2 tablespoon pumpkin pie spice
- 1/2 teaspoon vanilla extract
- 1/2 teaspoon baking powder
- 1/2 teaspoon salt
- 1 1/2 cups all-purpose flour
- 1/2 teaspoon baking soda

Cream Cheese Filling Ingredients:
- 1 (4 ounce package) cream cheese; softened
- 2 1/4 cups powdered sugar
- 1/2 cup butter; softened
- 1 teaspoon pure vanilla extract

Directions to Make the Cookies:
1. Grease the liner pan with some butter or spray it with some cooking spray.
2. Place the brown sugar and olive oil together in a bowl. Beat with an electronic beater until smooth.

3. Add in the egg and continue beating until the egg is well incorporated into the mix.
4. Add in the pumpkin puree, vanilla, baking soda, pumpkin pie spice, baking powder and salt. Continue whisking until it gets a light and fluffy texture.
5. Slowly fold using a silicon or rubber spatula. Do not over mix or the batter will fall flat.
6. Use a small cookie spoon or a round tablespoon and scoop the batter onto the greased liner pan. Leave about 2-inches of space between two cookies.
7. Place the Extender Ring on the base of your NuWave oven and cover with the dome.
8. Cook on the 'HI' setting for about 13 to 15 minutes or until the cookies spring back when touched lightly.
9. Let the cookies cool completely before filling them with the cream cheese filling.

Directions to Make the Cream Cheese Filling:
1. Place the cream cheese and butter in the bowl of an electric mixer.
2. Cream the butter and cream cheese together on the medium speed. Stop the mixer at regular interval so that you can scrape the sides of the bowl.
3. Add in the vanilla and continue whisking for another few minutes.
4. Lower the speed of the electric mixer and gradually add in the powdered sugar to the cream cheese and butter mix.
5. Continue beating until the mix is light and fluffy.
6. Spoon the cream cheese filling on the flat side of the cooled cookies. Top with another cookie and press down lightly to make a sandwich.
7. Serve immediately.

Note: If you do not have pumpkin pie spice mix handy, use the following recipe to make it at home by combining together:
- 3/4 teaspoon cinnamon
- 1/2 teaspoon ginger
- 1/2 teaspoon nutmeg
- 1/4 teaspoon allspice

192. Kids Favorite Chocolate Cake

Ingredients:
- 1 cup plain flour
- 1 cup sugar
- 1/2 cup cocoa
- 1 teaspoon baking powder
- 1 teaspoon baking soda
- 1/2 teaspoon salt
- 1 lightly beaten egg
- 1/2 cup milk
- 1/4 cup vegetable oil
- 1 teaspoon vanilla
- 1/2 cup boiling water
- Chocolate ganache
- 1 punnet of fresh raspberries

Instructions:
1. Sift dry ingredients into a medium size mixing bowl.
2. Add egg, milk, oil and vanilla.
3. With electric mixer beat mixture on medium speed for 2-3 minutes.

4. Stir in boiling water until well combined.
5. Pour mixture into 8" x 8" (20cm x 20cm) cake pan that has been oiled and lined with baking paper.
6. Bake in NuWave oven on 5cm rack for 30-35 minutes.
7. Cool in pan for 10 minutes; turn out onto cooling rack and allow to cool completely.
8. Coat cake with a thin layer of chocolate ganache, place fresh raspberries evenly over top of cake and drizzle the rest of the ganache over raspberries flicking spoon from side to side turning cake to ensure even coverage.

Chocolate Ganache
Ingredients:
- 2/3 cup thickened cream
- 7 oz. (200g) cooking chocolate

Instructions:
1. Place ingredients into a small saucepan.
2. Heat on medium heat until chocolate has melted and mixture is smooth.
3. Allow to cool for a few minutes and then pour gently over cake*.

*Use a biscuit tray under rack to catch spill over of ganache – this can be re-applied to cake.

193. Tasty Lemon Meringue Pie

Biscuit Pastry
Ingredients:
- 3 oz. (90g) butter
- 1/4 cup sugar
- 1 egg
- 1 1/4 cups plain flour
- 1/4 cup self raising flour

Instructions:
1. Beat butter until creamy, add sugar, beat until just combined.
2. Add beaten egg gradually; beating well after each addition. (Over creaming at this stage will make pastry difficult to handle.)
3. Work in 2/3 of the sifted flours with a wooden spoon, then remaining flour with the hand.
4. Turn on to lightly floured board, knead lightly until smooth. (Heavy handling of pastry will toughen it and make it difficult to roll.)
5. Wrap in plastic wrap and refrigerate for 30min before using.
6. Roll out and line a greased 23cm fluted pie pan with removable bottom with pastry. Refrigerate for further 30 mins before baking – this helps prevent shrinkage.
7. Bake in NuWave oven for 15min (10cm rack); remove and allow to cool.

Filling:
Ingredients:
- 4 tablespoon plain flour
- 4 tablespoon cornflour
- 2 teaspoon grated lemon rind
- 3/4 cup lemon juice
- 1 cup sugar
- 1 1/4 cups water
- 3 oz. (90g) butter
- 4 egg yolks

Instructions:
1. Combine sifted flours, lemon rind, lemon juice & sugar in saucepan. Add water, blend until smooth, stir over heat until mixture boils and thickens; this is important, the mixture must boil. Reduce heat; stir a further 2 mins.
2. Remove from heat; stir in butter and lightly beaten egg-yolks, stir until butter has melted; cool.
3. Spread cold lemon filling evenly into pastry case.

Meringue:

Ingredients:
- 4 egg whites
- 2 tablespoon water
- Pinch salt
- 3/4 cup caster sugar

Instructions:
1. Combine egg-whites, water and salt in small bowl of electric mixer.
2. Beat on high until soft peaks form. Gradually add sugar, beat well until sugar has dissolved. (Approx 15 mins)
3. Spoon on top of lemon filling spreading meringue to edges of pie to seal; peak meringue decoratively with knife.
4. Bake in NuWave oven with extender ring fitted, on 5cm rack, level 8, for 15mins or until golden brown.

194. Tasty Cherry Galette

Ingredients:
- 1.7 oz. (50g) butter; softened
- 2 tablespoon caster sugar
- 1 egg yolk
- 1/2 cup (60g) almond meal
- 1 tablespoon self-raising flour
- 4 sheets filo pastry
- 1 oz. (30g) butter; melted
- 7 oz. (200g) frozen pitted cherries
- 2 teaspoon icing sugar

Instructions:
1. Beat softened butter, sugar and egg yolk with electric mixer 4mins or until light and fluffy. Stir in flour and almond meal.
2. Brush filo sheets with melted butter and fold in half. Stack sheets on top of each other on baking paper.
3. Spread almond mixture over pastry leaving a 4cm border.
4. Press frozen cherries into almond mixture. Fold the pastry edges in to make border.
5. Bake in NuWave oven; on 5cm rack, level 10, for 18mins.
6. Sprinkle with sifted icing sugar to serve. Great with ice-cream!

195. Cranberry and Apple Turnovers

Ingredients:
- 1 X 14 oz. (400g) can pie apples
- 1/3 cup dried cranberries
- 4 tablespoon hazelnut meal
- 2 tablespoon caster sugar

- 2 sheets puff pastry
- extra caster sugar
- egg white

Instructions:
1. Mix together apples, cranberries, hazelnut meal and caster sugar until combined.
2. Cut pastry sheets into four.
3. Divide mixture between each quarter, placing mixture on one side leaving 20mm edge.
4. Brush edges of pastry with egg white, fold pastry over and seal with a fork.
5. Cut three slits in top of turnover, brush top with egg white and sprinkle with extra sugar.
6. Bake in NuWave oven on 10cm rack for 10 minutes; turn pastries over and cook for another 5 minutes.

Tip: Spray racks with oil or place pastries on pieces of baking paper until turned over.

196. Polenta Syrup and Orange Cake

Ingredients:
- 1 cup caster sugar
- 3 eggs
- 3/4 cup extra-light olive oil
- 1 tablespoon orange rind; finely grated
- 1/4 cup orange juice
- 1 1/2 cups self-raising flour; sifted
- 1/2 cup polenta
- 1/3 cup almond meal (ground almonds)
- 2 tablespoon flaked almonds

Instructions:
1. Grease and line with baking paper, a 20cm spring-form pan or ring pan.
2. Whisk sugar, eggs, oil, orange rind and orange juice together in a bowl until smooth.
3. Add flour, polenta and almond meal. Stir to combine.
4. Pour into prepared pan and top with flaked almonds.
5. Bake in NuWave oven on 5cm rack, level 9, for 45 minutes or inserted skewer comes out clean.

Cover with baking paper if over-browning during cooking. Stand in pan for 5 minutes. Turn out onto wire rack over baking tray.

Make orange syrup:

Ingredients:
- 1 1/4 cups caster sugar
- 1/2 cup orange juice
- 1 cup cold water

Instructions:
1. Combine sugar, orange juice and water in a saucepan over medium heat. Cook, stirring, for 2-3 minutes or until sugar has dissolved. Bring to a simmer. Simmer, without stirring, for 5 minutes or until thickened. Transfer to a heatproof jug.
2. Pour half of the hot syrup over hot cake.
3. Allow to stand for 15-20 minutes to slightly cool.
4. Serve cake with remaining syrup.

197. Fruit Kebabs With Orange Sauce and Passionfruit

Ingredients:
- 1/2 cup water
- 1/4 cup orange juice
- 1/2 cup caster sugar
- 1 tablespoon honey
- 1/2 cup passionfruit pulp
- 2 tablespoons orange flavored liqueur; optional
- 1 small pineapple; chopped coarsely
- 1 small pawpaw; chopped coarsely
- 2 large bananas; sliced thickly
- 8.8 oz. (250g) strawberries
- You will need about six passionfruit for this recipe or canned passionfruit pulp works just as well.
- Cointreau or Grand Marnier makes the sauce exquisite!

Instructions:
1. To make sauce, combine water, juice, sugar and honey in a small saucepan.
2. Stir over heat, without boiling, until sugar dissolves; then bring to the boil. Reduce heat; simmer, without stirring, about 10 minutes or until mixture thickens slightly.
3. Remove from heat; stir in passionfruit pulp and liqueur, cool sauce 5 minutes.
4. Meanwhile; thread fruit onto skewers and brush with passionfruit sauce.
5. Place kebabs in NuWave oven on 10cm rack and balance of passionfruit sauce in ovenproof dish on liner tray and cook for 8 minutes.
6. Serve kebabs drizzled with warm passionfruit/orange sauce and ice cream.

198. Sweet Hot Cross Bun Pudding

Ingredients:
- 6 hot cross buns
- 1/4 cup white choc bits
- 1cup milk
- 1cup thin cream
- 5 eggs
- 1/4 cup caster sugar
- 1/2 teaspoon vanilla extract
- 1/4 cup dark choc bits
- 1/4 cup slivered almonds

Instructions:
1. Grease a 22cm pie-dish (or shallow casserole dish) and line bottom with baking paper.
2. Slice hot cross buns into six slices; discarding the dark ends.
3. Using half of the slices; line base of tin fitting them in snugly.
4. Sprinkle over the white choc bits.
5. Whisk eggs, milk, cream, sugar and vanilla together in a large jug.
6. Pour half the mixture over buns.
7. Top with remaining slices; pour over rest of egg mixture.
8. Allow to stand for 30 mins.
9. Top with dark choc bits and slivered almonds and bake in NuWave oven, 5cm rack; level 8 for 50-55 mins until set and brown (it will rise when cooked and drop down on cooling).

10. Cool completely in tin. Run knife around edge of pudding and turn onto plate. Remove paper and invert pudding onto serving plate.
11. Cut into wedges to serve.

199. Delicious Profiteroles

Ingredients:
- 2.6 oz. (75g) butter; chopped
- 1 cup water
- 1 cup plain flour
- 4 eggs

Instructions:
1. Combine butter and water in saucepan; bring to the boil.
2. When butter is melted and water boiling rapidly, add sifted flour all at once: stir vigorously until mixture leaves side of saucepan and forms a smooth ball.
3. Transfer mixture to small bowl of electric mixer, add eggs one at a time, beating well after each addition. Mixture should be glossy.
4. Cover 5cm rack with baking paper and drop teaspoonoonfuls of mixture about 5cm apart.
5. Bake in NuWave oven; level 10, for 20 minutes, turning over after 10mins.
6. When timer goes off; open oven and cut a slit in side of each puff.
7. Bake in NuWave oven; on level 7, for a further 5 minutes to dry puffs out.
8. Place on cooling rack and allow to cool. When cold, fill each puff with custard/cream in a piping bag and top with chocolate sauce.

Custard Cream:

Ingredients:
- 2 level tablespoon custard powder
- 1 tablespoon sugar
- 1 cup milk
- 1 teaspoon vanilla extract
- 300ml carton double cream
- 1 tablespoon icing sugar

Instructions:
1. Mix custard powder, sugar and enough of the milk to make a runny paste.
2. Bring milk to the boil. Remove from heat and whisk in custard paste.
3. Return to the heat and bring back to a simmer until thick (this custard will be thicker than normal as we are only using half the quantity of milk).
4. Remove from heat and allow to cool to room temperature.
5. Meanwhile; whip double cream with icing sugar and vanilla until thick and mix into cold custard.

Chocolate Sauce:

Ingredients:
- 7 oz. (200g) dark cooking chocolate
- 3/4 cup cream
- 1/2 teaspoon vanilla extract
- 2 tablespoon Crème de Cocao liqueur

Instructions:
1. Place chocolate and cream in a small saucepan and stir over a medium heat until chocolate has melted and combined.

2. Remove from heat.
3. Add vanilla and liqueur and stir until combined.

200. Amazingly Easy Two-Egg Pavlova

Ingredients:
- 2 egg-whites
- 1 1/2 cups caster sugar
- 1/2 teaspoon vanilla
- 1 teaspoon vinegar
- 1 teaspoon cornflour
- 4 tablespoon boiling water

Instructions:
1. Place all ingredients into small bowl of electric mixer, beat on high speed until mixture is very stiff (approx 15min).
2. Spread onto prepared baking paper on 5cm rack.
3. Bake in NuWave oven; power level 8, with extender ring added, for 40 minutes.
4. Allow to cool in oven with dome propped open about 1cm (I use a spoon to do this).

201. Blueberry Muffins

Ingredients:
- 1 cup fresh blueberries
- 2 tablespoon margarine
- 1 cup all-purpose flour; divided
- 3/4 cup white sugar
- ½ teaspoon vanilla extract
- 1 egg
- ½-cup milk
- ½ teaspoon salt
- 2 teaspoon baking powder

Instructions:
1. Sprinkle about 2 tablespoon of the flour over the blueberries and toss well until the blueberries are well coated in the flour.
2. In a separate mixing bowl; place the margarine. Slowly add in the sugar and whisk well until the margarine is creamed.
3. Add the eggs to the margarine mixture and whisk well until just combined.
4. Pour in the vanilla extract and mix well.
5. Add in the milk and whisk well. Keep aside.
6. Sieve together the flour, salt and baking powder in a small mixing bowl.
7. Pour the dry ingredients into the wet ingredients and fold until all the ingredients are well combined and there are no lumps in the batter.
8. Add the flour covered blueberries to the batter and fold.
9. Fill 12 silicone cupcake liners with the batter until they are about 2/3 full.
10. Place the muffins on the 1-inch cooking rack and bake at 350 degrees Fahrenheit for about 15 to 20 minutes or until a knife run through the center of the muffin comes clean.
11. Cool the cupcakes on a wire rack before serving.

202. Delicious Cinnamon Apple Filo Pastries

Ingredients:
- 6 sheets filo pastry*
- 0.8 oz. (25g) unsalted butter; melted
- 2 Granny Smith apples; cored, peeled, halved and thinly sliced
- 2 tablespoon caster sugar
- 1/2 teaspoon cinnamon

Instructions:
1. Lay a sheet of filo pastry on the work surface, brush it with a little of the melted butter, then lay another sheet on top. Continue brushing with butter and layering until all six filo sheets are stacked on top of each other.
2. Using a 12cm / 41/2in saucer as a guide, cut out four pastry rounds with a sharp knife.
3. Brush each pastry round with the remaining butter and place them on baking paper.
4. Arrange the apple slices on the pastry rounds, fanning them out from the center. Dust with sugar and cinnamon.
5. Bake in the NuWave oven on 10cm rack; level 10 for 12 minutes; or until the pastry is golden and the apples are tender.
6. Serve with icecream or cream as desired.

*Allow filo pastry to sit in packet at room temperature for 2 hours before handling – otherwise the pastry will crack and break where there are chilled bits!

203. My Favorite Plum Tart

Ingredients:
- 4.5 oz. (125g) butter
- 3.8 oz. (110g) caster sugar
- 3 small eggs or 2 large eggs
- 1/4 teaspoon cinnamon
- 1/2 teaspoon vanilla essence
- Grated zest 1/3 orange
- 8 – 10 blood plums
- 3.5 oz. 100g self raising flour
- 4 tablespoon. (25g) ground almonds

Instructions:
1. Cream together the butter and caster sugar until light and creamy, add the eggs, beating well between each addition.
2. Fold in the flour, ground almonds, vanilla essence, orange zest and cinnamon.
3. Pour into a buttered 23cm flan tin and arrange the plum halves on top.
4. Bake in NuWave oven with extender ring fitted, on 5cm rack; level 10 for 35-40mins.
5. Serve with a generous scoop of vanilla bean ice-cream or a dollop of clotted cream.

204. Popular Portuguese Custard Tarts

Ingredients:
- 3 egg yolks
- 1/2 cup caster sugar
- 2 tablespoon cornflour
- 3/4 cup cream
- 1/2 cup water
- strip of lemon rind
- 2 teaspoon vanilla essence
- 1 sheet frozen ready-rolled puff pastry

Instructions:
1. Grease 2 x 6-hole muffin pans.
2. Whisk egg yolks, sugar and corn-flour in medium saucepan until combined. Gradually whisk in cream and water until smooth. Add lemon rind, stir over medium heat until mixture boils and thickens.
3. Remove pan from heat; remove and discard rind, stir in vanilla essence. Cover surface of custard with plastic wrap, cool.
4. Cut pastry sheet in half. Stack the two halves on top of each other. Stand about 5mins or until thawed. Roll the pastry up tightly from the short side, then cut the log into twelve 1cm rounds. Lay pastry, cut-side up, on a floured surface, roll each round out to about 10cm (turning pastry as you go to keep round shape). Press rounds into the prepared muffin pans with your fingers.
5. Spoon cooled custard into pastry cases.
6. Bake in NuWave oven on 5cm rack; level 10 for 20mins. Remove tarts from pan and place directly back onto rack and bake a further 5mins.

205. Granny Smith Apple Sponge Pudding

Ingredients:
- 8 Granny Smith apples; peeled & cored (4 apples chopped and 2 thinly sliced)
- 1/2 cup caster sugar
- 1 teaspoon grated lemon rind
- 1/4 cup water
- 2 eggs
- 1/3 cup caster sugar; extra
- 2 tablespoon cornflour
- 2 tablespoon plain flour
- 2 tablespoon self-raising flour

Instructions:
1. Combine apples, sugar, rind and water in saucepan, bring to boil, reduce heat, simmer, covered, for about 15 minutes or until tender.
2. Pour hot apple mixture into a deep, greased, ovenproof dish (6 cup capacity).
3. Beat eggs in a small bowl with electric mixer until thick and creamy.
4. Gradually add extra sugar, beating until dissolved between each addition.
5. Sift flours over egg mixture and fold through gently.
6. Spread mixture evenly over hot apple mixture.
7. Bake in NuWave oven on 5cm rack; level 10 for 20-25mins.

Note: Sensational served with custard, cream or ice-cream! A nice alternative is to replace 6 of the apples with choppe rhubarb. You will need about 425g or 5 cups rhubarb.

206. Nuwave Style Queen Puddings

Ingredients:
- 2 cups (140g) stale breadrumbs
- 1 tablespoon caster sugar
- 1 teaspoon vanilla extract
- 1 teaspoon finely grated lemon rind
- 2 1/2 cups (625ml) milk
- 2 oz. (60g) butter
- 4 eggs; separated
- 1/4 cup (80g) raspberry jam; warmed
- 3/4 cup (165g) castor sugar; extra
- Grease 6 x 3/4 cup (180ml) ovenproof ramekins.

Instructions:
1. Combine breadcrumbs, sugar, vanilla and rind in a large bowl.
2. Heat milk and butter in a medium saucepan until almost boiling, pour over bread mixture, stand 10 minutes.
3. Stir in yolks.
4. Divide mixture among ramekins.
5. Bake in NuWave oven; on 5cm rack, level 10, for 20mins.
6. Gently spread tops of puddings with warm jam.
7. Beat egg whites in a small bowl with electric mixer until soft peaks form, gradually add extra sugar, beating until sugar dissolves.
8. Spoon meringue over puddings and bake in NuWave oven; 5cm rack, extender ring added for a further 10mins.

207. Delicious Classic Pavlova

Ingredients:
- 5 egg whites
- 1 1/4 cups caster sugar
- 1 1/2 teaspoon vanilla
- 1 1/2 teaspoon white vinegar
- 1 1/2 tablespoon corn flour
- Pinch salt

Instructions:
1. Beat egg whites until stiff.
2. Add caster sugar slowly and then salt.
3. Beat for a further 5 minutes until thick, stiff peaks form.
4. Beat in vanilla and vinegar; then fold in corn flour.
5. Spoon mixture onto baking paper with a 20cm circle drawn onto it and pile meringue high.
6. Bake in NuWave oven; with extender ring attached on 5cm rack, level 6 for 35 minutes.
7. Allow to cool in oven by propping open the dome about 2cm.
8. Top with whipped cream, fresh strawberries, kiwi fruit, sliced banana and passion fruit.

208. Amazing Bourbon, Caramel Pudding

Ingredients:
- 2 stale croissants
- 3.5 oz. (100g) caster sugar
- 2 tablespoon water
- 125ml double cream
- 125ml full-fat milk
- 2 tablespoon bourbon
- 2 eggs; beaten

Instructions:
1. Tear croissants into pieces and put in a small gratin dish (about 500ml capacity).
2. Place caster sugar and water in a saucepan, swirl around to help dissolve sugar before putting pan on medium – high heat.
3. Caramelise the sugar and water mixture by letting it bubble away, without stirring, until it all turns a deep amber colour – this will take around 3-5 minutes. Keep looking but don't be too timid!
4. Turn down heat to low. Add cream, whisking away, milk and bourbon.
5. Take off the heat and still whisking, add beaten eggs.
6. Pour custard over croissants and leave to steep for 10 minutes.
7. Bake in NuWave oven on 5cm rack; level 10 for 10 minutes, add extender ring and bake a further 10 minutes

209. Nuwave Style Baked Rice Puddings

Ingredients:
- 2 cups milk
- 300ml thin cream
- 1/2 cup medium grain (calrose) rice; rinsed, drained
- 1/2 cup caster sugar
- 1 cinnamon stick
- 1 vanilla bean; split, seeds scraped
- Pinch ground nutmeg; plus extra to sprinkle
- 2 strips lemon rind
- 2 egg yolks

Instructions:
1. Combine milk, cream, rice, sugar, cinnamon, vanilla bean and seeds, nutmeg and lemon rind in a medium saucepan. Cook over medium heat; stirring occasionally, for 5 minutes or until it reaches a simmer. Remove from heat and set aside for 15 minutes to infuse.
2. Put rice mixture through a sieve. Remove and discard the cinnamon stick, lemon rind and vanill bean. Equally divide rice into casserole dishes.
3. Add egg yolks to milk mixture and whisk to combine.
4. Pour milk mixture equally into 4 x 1-cup casserole dishes over rice.
5. Bake in NuWave oven with extender ring fitted; power level 10, on 5cm rack for 10mins. Stir and sprinkle with extra nutmeg; bake a further 30mins or until rice is tender and custard is set.
6. Remove from oven and allow to stand for 10 minutes before serving.
7. Serve warm with stewed fruit.

210. Mouthwatering Hummingbird Muffins With Creamed Honey Spread

Ingredients:
- 1 1/4 self raising flour
- 1/2 teaspoon cinnamon
- 1/2 cup caster sugar
- 1 egg; lightly beaten
- 1/4 cup olive oil
- 1/2 cup walnuts; chopped
- 1 ripe banana; mashed
- 7.5 oz. (220g) can crushed pineapple in juice
- 1 small can of pineapple pieces (for decoration only)

Instructions:
1. Sift flour and cinnamon into a large bowl and stir in sugar. Add egg, oil, walnuts, banana and pineapple and stir until mixture is just combined.
2. Spoon mixture into greased 6-hole muffin pan or silicone individual muffin pans to 2/3 of the way up the sides. Top each muffin with a piece of pineapple.
3. Bake in NuWave oven on 5cm rack; level 10 for 20mins; allow to cool in pan/s.
4. When cold; dust muffins with icing sugar and serve with a generous dollop of Creamed Honey Spread.

Creamed Honey Spread

Ingredients:
- 8.8 oz. (250g) light cream cheese; chopped
- 2 tablespoon icing sugar
- 1/4 cup creamed honey

Instructions:
Place all ingredients into a bowl and beat with a spoon until smooth. Refrigerate.

211. Orange Glazed Carrot Cake

Ingredients:
- 1 ¼-cups all-purpose flour
- 1/8 teaspoon ground nutmeg
- ½ teaspoon baking soda
- 1/8 teaspoon salt
- 1 teaspoon baking powder
- 3/4 teaspoon cinnamon
- 1/8 teaspoon ground cloves
- ¼-cup vegetable oil
- 1 cup packed light brown sugar
- 1 egg at room temperature
- ½ teaspoon vanilla extract
- 1/6 cup unsweetened applesauce
- Zest from ½ orange
- 1 cup grated carrots
- 1 – 1 ½ tablespoon fresh orange juice
- ½-cup confections sugar; sifted

Optional Ingredients:
- 1/6 cup chopped pecans
- ¼-cup raisins

Instructions:
1. Add the flour, baking soda, cinnamon, cloves, baking powder, salt and nutmeg to a large mixing bowl. Mix well until all the ingredients are well combined. Keep aside.

2. In another large mixing bowl, place the brown sugar, egg, vanilla, oil, applesauce and orange zest together. Whisk well until all the ingredients are well combined.
3. Pour the dry ingredients into the wet ingredient in parts, mixing well after each addition to ensure that all the dry ingredients are well incorporated.
4. Add the raisins, carrots and pecans to the batter and fold until just combined. Do not over mix.
5. Grease a 4-inch by 4-inch baking pan with some butter.
6. Pour the prepared cake batter into the greased baking pan.
7. Place the prepared baking pan on the 1-inch cooking rack.
8. Bake for about 40 to 45 minutes at 375 degrees Fahrenheit. Check if the cake is done by poking a toothpick in the center of the cake; if it comes out clean, the cake is done cooking.
9. While the cake bakes; pour the orange juice in a small mixing bowl.
10. Add the powdered sugar to the orange juice and whisk well until combined.
11. Once the cake is done; cool it in the pan for about 5 minutes before cooling it on a wire rack.
12. Pour the prepared orange glaze over the cooled cake and serve.

212. Lemon and Poppy Seed Glazed Cookies

Ingredients to Make the Cookies:
- 1 cup sifted flour
- 1/4 teaspoon salt
- 1/4 teaspoon baking powder
- 1/4 cup confectioners' sugar
- 1/2 cup (1 stick) unsalted butter

Ingredients to Make the Glaze:
- 1/2 cup confectioners' sugar
- 1/2 tablespoon fresh lemon juice
- 2 tablespoons heavy cream
- 1/2 teaspoon poppy seeds

Directions to Make the Cookies:
1. Sieve the flour, salt and baking powder together in a bowl and keep aside.
2. Place the butter in a small bowl and cream with an electronic beater until light and fluffy.
3. Slowly add the sugar to the butter and continue beating until all the sugar is incorporated and the mix is light in texture.
4. Gradually pour the dry ingredients into the creamed butter mix and continue blending until all the dry ingredients are incorporated into the butter mix.
5. Oil your hands and roll balls about 1-inch balls from the dough.
6. Arrange the balls on a flat cookie sheet in a single layer and refrigerate for about 20 to 25 minutes.
7. Place the dough balls in a single layer on the 1-inch rack and bake on the 'HI' setting for about 12 to 15 minutes.
8. If all the dough balls do not fit on the rack in one go, you might have to bake the cookies in multiple batches.
9. Transfer the baked cookies onto a wire rack and cool to room temperature before glazing.

Directions to Make the Glaze:
1. Place the confectioners' sugar, lemon juice and cream together in a mixing bowl. Whisk until well combined.
2. Add in the poppy seeds and mix well until well incorporated.
3. Once the cookies have cooled; drizzle the prepared glaze over the cookies or dip the top halves of the cookies directly into the glaze.
4. Let the glaze set on the cookies for about 15 to 20 minutes before serving.

213. Delicious Chocolate Topped Oat Cookies

Ingredients:
- 6 tablespoons quick-cooking oats
- 6 tablespoons granulated sugar
- 6 tablespoons all-purpose flour
- 1/2 teaspoon ground cinnamon
- 6 tablespoons teaspoon chili powder
- 1/4 teaspoon salt
- 1/4 teaspoon baking soda
- 15 tablespoons melted unsalted butter
- 3/4 cups sliced almonds
- 2 tablespoons half and half cream or whole milk
- 1/2 teaspoon pure vanilla extract
- 2 tablespoons light corn syrup
- 2 ounces fine-quality bittersweet chocolate; chopped

Instructions:
1. Place the oats, sugar, chili powder, salt, flour, cinnamon and baking soda together in a large mixing bowl. Whisk well until combined.
2. Add in the almonds and keep aside.
3. Combine the half and half (or milk if using), vanilla extract and corn syrup together in another bowl. Whisk until all the ingredients are well combined.
4. Pour the wet ingredients into the dry ingredients gradually. Fold gently to form a smooth, lump free batter.
5. Grease the liner pan with some butter or spray with some cooking spray.
6. Scoop the batter onto the greased liner pan, leaving about 3-inches between two cookies.
7. Bake on the '9' setting of your NuWave oven for about 14 to 15 minutes or until the cookies look dried out and crisp around the edges.
8. Place a wire rack on a parchment sheet. This will ensure that you do not create a large mess when you drizzle the chocolate over the cookies.
9. Gently transfer the cookies to a wire rack and cool to room temperature.
10. While the cookies cool, melt the chocolate over a double boiler of simmering water or microwave for 30-second intervals until the chocolate is completely liquidated.
11. Use a spoon to drip the melted chocolate over the cookies and make a variety of patterns on the cookies.
12. Serve after the chocolate has cooled and solidified.

214. Delicious Dense Pound Cake

Ingredients:
- 3 cups all-purpose flour
- 1/2 teaspoon salt
- 1/2 teaspoon baking powder
- 1 cup (about 2 sticks) unsalted butter; softened
- 2 teaspoons pure vanilla extract
- 3 cups sugar
- 1 cup heavy cream
- 6 large eggs

Instructions:
1. Sift the flour, salt and baking powder together in a sieve and keep aside.
2. Place the butter and sugar together in the bowl of an electrical mixer. Beat on the medium high speed until it gets creamy and fluffy.
3. Pour in the vanilla extract and continue beating for another minute.
4. Add in the eggs, one at a time, and beat well until the egg gets incorporated into the batter before adding in another egg.
5. Slowly add in the flour mix to the electric mixer bowl; alternating with heavy cream. Make sure you start and end with the flour. This ensures that your cake remains moist.
6. Grease a silicon Bundt pan with some butter or spray it with some cooking spray. Lightly flour the pan.
7. Pour the batter into the prepared Bundt pan.
8. Place the batter filled Bundt pan on a 1-inch rack.
9. Place the extender Ring on the base of your NuWave oven.
10. Bake on the '8' setting of your NuWave oven for about 45 to 50 minutes. Do not open the dome of the oven while the cake bakes or else the cake will become hard and dry.
11. Reduce the temperature setting to the '7' mark and still do not open the dome.
12. Once the timer is up; open the dome and insert a skewer in the center of the cake.
13. If the skewer does not come out clean; bake for another 5 minutes, but do not bake for more than 5 minutes.
14. Remove the cake from the oven and cool in the pan for about 15 minutes.
15. Invert the cake onto a serving plate and cut into slices.
16. Serve warm topped with some chocolate sauce or marmalade and with a side of ice cream.

215. Butter and Bread Pudding

Ingredients:
- 6 thin slices white bread; crust removed
- 1.5 oz. (40g) butter
- 3 eggs
- 1/4 cup caster sugar
- 2 cups milk
- 1 teaspoon vanilla essence
- 1/2 cup sultanas
- Nutmeg or cinnamon

Instructions:
1. Sprinkle sultanas over base of extender dish.

2. Butter bread and cut into triangles. Arrange in bottom of extender dish (single layer but overlapping slightly) butter side up.
3. Whisk eggs, sugar, milk and essence together in bowl. Pour half the custard mixture over bread, stand for 10 minutes.
4. Whisk remaining egg mixture again; pour into dish.
5. Sprinkle with nutmeg or cinnamon.
6. Place on 5cm rack and bake in NuWave oven; power level 8, for 30 minutes, or until custard is set.

216. Nuwave Style Baked Filled Peach Halves

Ingredients:
- 6 slip-stone peaches; halved with stone removed
- 1/4 cup sultanas
- 1/4 cup slivered almonds
- 2 almond macaroons; crushed
- 2 tablespoon brown sugar
- 1/4 cup honey

Instructions:
1. Mix together sultanas, slivered almonds, macaroons and brown sugar until combined.
2. Fill each peach half with mixture, piling it as high as it will hold and dividing the mixture evenly among the peaches.
3. Drizzle honey over the topping of each peach until filling is well coated.
4. Bake in NuWave oven; on 5cm rack for 15mins or until peaches are cooked through (test with skewer).
5. Serve with custard, double cream or ice-cream and sprinkled with additional crushed macaroons.

217. Chocolate Cake (Egg less)

Ingredients:
- 1 1/2 cups plain flour
- 1 cup sugar
- 4 tablespoon cocoa
- 1 teaspoon bicarbonate of soda
- 1/2 teaspoon salt
- 1 cup water
- 1/3 cup vegetable oil
- 2 tablespoon white vinegar
- 2 teaspoon vanilla extract

Instructions:
1. Sift the dry ingredients into a bowl.
2. Combine wet ingredients and stir into flour mixture.
3. Pour mixture into greased mini muffin pans (I use my individual silicone ones); place on 5cm rack and bake in NuWave oven for 10 minutes (mini); 20 minutes (muffin). Cool on wire racks.

218. Honey and Cinnamon Crackers

Ingredients:
- 1 ½ tablespoon whole milk
- ½ tablespoon pure vanilla extract
- 1 tablespoon honey
- ½-cups all-purpose flour
- 1/8 cup granulated sugar
- 1/6 cup firmly packed dark brown sugar
- ¼-teaspoon baking soda
- 1/8 teaspoon salt
- 1/8 teaspoon ground cinnamon
- 2 tablespoon unsalted butter; cut into 1/2-inch cubes and frozen

Instructions:
1. Place the honey, milk and vanilla extract together in a small mixing bowl. Whisk well until all the ingredients are well emulsified and forma smooth mix. Keep aside.
2. Mix together the flour, baking soda, salt, sugar and cinnamon together into the jar of a food processor. Blitz until all the ingredients are well combined together.
3. Add the frozen butter pieces to the flour mix and continue blitzing until the mix has crumbly texture.
4. Slowly pour the milk mixture into the flour mix and continue blitzing it gets a doughy texture.
5. Remove the dough from the food processor and place on a flat, lightly floured work surface.
6. Cover the dough with plastic wrap and flatten the dough into a flat disk.
7. Refrigerate the dough for about 40 to 45 minutes.
8. Once the dough is chilled, remove the plastic wrap and transfer the dough on a flat work surface. Make sure you dust the surface with some floor.
9. Roll the dough until it is about 1/8-inch thick.
10. To the 3-inch cooking rack, add the silicone baking ring.
11. Use cookie cutters to cut the dough into desired shapes and transfer the cookies to the silicone baking ring.
12. Bake the cookies for about 8 to 10 minutes at 300 degrees Fahrenheit.
13. Cool the cookies in the tray for about 3 minutes before transferring them to a wire rack to cool.
14. Repeat with the leftover dough. Serve warm if possible.

219. Chocolate Chip Oatmeal Cookies

Ingredients:
- 1 ¼-cups old fashioned oats
- ¼-cup granulated sugar
- 1 cup all-purpose flour
- ½-cup brown sugar
- ½ teaspoon baking soda
- ½ teaspoon salt
- ½-cup melted coconut oil
- 2 teaspoon vanilla extract
- 1 large egg
- ½-cup plain candy coated chocolate pieces
- ½-cup chocolate chips

Instructions:
1. Combine the oats, granulated sugar, flour, brown sugar, baking soda and salt together in a large mixing bowl. Mix well until all the ingredients are well combined. Keep aside.
2. In a separate large bowl; pour in the oil, vanilla extract and egg. Whisk well until all the ingredients are well emulsified.
3. Slowly add the flour mix to the wet ingredients in 3 parts, mixing thoroughly after each addition to ensure that there are no lumps.
4. Add in the candy coated chocolate pieces and the chocolate chips to the batter. Fold until just combined.
5. On the 2-inch cooking rack; place a silicone baking ring.
6. Add the Extender Ring to the base of your oven.
7. Use a 1-inch cookie scoop to scoop out dough balls and place them at 1-inch intervals on the silicone baking ring.
8. Bake the cookies at 300 degrees Fahrenheit for about 14 to 16 minutes or until the cookies are light brown on the top.
9. Repeat the baking process until all the cookies are baked.
10. Cool the cookies completely before serving.

220. Easy Plum Crumbles

Ingredients:
- 1.5 oz. (40g) butter; chopped
- 1/4 cup self raising flour
- 2 tablespoon brown sugar
- 1/3 cup rolled oats
- 1/4 cup macadamia nuts; chopped
- 29 oz. (825g) can whole plums; drained, halved, stones removed
- 1 cup vanilla yoghurt
- 1/2 teaspoon mixed spice

Instructions:
1. Combine flour and sugar in a medium bowl. Add butter. Using fingertips, rub butter into flour mixture until mixture resembles breadcrumbs.
2. Stir in oats and macadamias.
3. Divide plums between 4 x greased ramekins (1 cup capacity). Sprinkle flour mixture over plums.
4. Stir in cheese with a wooden spoon.
5. Bake in NuWave oven on 5cm rack; level 10, for 15 minutes, until plums are hot and top is golden.
6. Meanwhile; combine yoghurt and mixed spice in a bowl. Serve crumble with spiced yoghurt.

221. Banana Pineapple Nut Bread

Ingredients:
- 3 cups all-purpose flour
- 3/4 teaspoon salt
- 1 teaspoon baking soda
- 2 cups white sugar
- 1 teaspoon ground cinnamon
- 1 cup walnuts; chopped
- 3 eggs; lightly beaten
- 1 cup vegetable oil
- 4 ripe bananas; mashed
- 1 (8 ounce) can crushed pineapple; drained
- 2 teaspoons vanilla extract

Instructions:
1. Spray two 9 x 5-inch loaf pans with cooking spray.
2. In large mixing bowl; combine flour, salt, baking soda, sugar, and cinnamon. Add in walnuts, eggs, oil, banana, pineapple, and vanilla. Stir until just blended. Pour batter into pans.
3. Place pans on 1-inch rack and bake on High power (350 degrees F) for 45-50 minutes or until toothpick inserted in center comes out clean. Let rest under dome for 1-2 minutes before removing from NuWave Oven. Cool before slicing.

222. Salted Chocolate Tart

Ingredients:
- 1 cup crushed sea salt potato chips
- 3 tablespoons melted unsalted butter
- 2 tablespoons all-purpose flour
- 10 tablespoons heavy cream; divided
- 1/2 teaspoon vanilla extract
- 5 ounces semisweet chocolate morsels
- 1/4 teaspoon salt
- 4 ounces bittersweet chocolate morsels
- 1 large egg
- Sea salt for garnish

Instructions:
1. Place the crushed sea salt flavored potato chips, flour and melted butter together in the jar of a blender or food processor. Blitz for about a minute until all the ingredients are well combined.
2. Lightly grease a spring form pan with some butter or spray with some cooking spray.
3. Press the prepared chip and melted butter mixture in the bottom and over the sides of the greased spring form pan.
4. Place the spring form pan on a 3-inch rack and bake on the 'HI' setting for about 5 minutes until the crust hardens.
5. Remove the crust from the oven and keep aside until cooled to room temperature.
6. Pour about 2 tablespoons of the heavy whipping cream into a small saucepan. Heat over a medium low flame until the heavy cream is just lightly bubbling.
7. Reduce the flame to a low and add the semisweet chocolate morsels to the cream. Gently mix using a rubber spatula until the chocolate melts and becomes smooth. Take off heat.
8. Add in the salt and vanilla to the chocolate mix. Mix well.

9. Add the eggs one by one to the chocolate mix and mix well until the egg is incorporated; before adding another egg.
10. Pour the prepared salted chocolate mix onto the prepared crust and tap lightly against the kitchen counter to ensure that there are no air bubbles.
11. Place the Extender Ring on the base of your NuWave oven and place the spring form pan on the 1-inch rack.
12. Bake on the '8' setting for about 16 to 18 minutes.
13. Increase the temperature setting to '9' and bake for another 10 minutes.
14. Remove the pan from the oven and cool for a few minutes.
15. While the pie cools; prepare the ganache.
16. Heat the remaining heavy whipping cream on a medium high flame in a saucepan until lightly bubbling.
17. Take the saucepan off the heat and add the bittersweet chocolate morsels to the warm cream.
18. Mix well until smooth.
19. Once the pie is cooled, pour the prepared ganache over it. Use a spatula to make an even layer.
20. Refrigerate for 8 to 10 hours or until overnight.
21. Cut into slices and serve topped with a pinch of sea salt.

223. Coconut and Raspberry Muffins

Ingredients:
- 2 1/2 cups self raising flour
- 3 oz. (90g) butter; chopped
- 1 cup caster sugar
- 1 1/4 cups buttermilk
- 1 egg; lightly beaten
- 1/3 cup desiccated coconut
- 5.2 oz. (150g) fresh or frozen raspberries
- 2 tablespoon shredded coconut

Instructions:
1. Place flour in a large bowl; rub in butter (alternatively, process flour & butter in food processor).
2. Stir in sugar, buttermilk, egg, desiccated coconut and raspberries until just combined – do not over-mix!
3. Divide mixture among holes of 2 greased 6 hole muffin pans or 12 silicone muffins holders and sprinkle with shredded coconut.
4. Bake in NuWave oven; 5cm rack for 15-18mins or until muffin springs back when lightly pressed.
5. Stand muffins in pan for 5mins before turning out onto wire rack to cool.

224. Mix Berry Cream Pie

Ingredients:
- 1 unbaked 5-inch pastry shell (packaged or home cooked)
- ½-cup granulated sugar
- ½-cup flour
- Pinch of salt
- ¼-teaspoon vanilla extract
- ½-cup sour cream
- ¼-teaspoon almond extract
- ½ (6 ounce) container fresh raspberries
- ½ (1 pound) container fresh strawberries
- ½ (6 ounce) container fresh blackberries

Instructions:
1. Place the readymade or homemade piecrust on the 4-inch cooking rack.
2. Bake the piecrust on the HI power setting for about 20 to 25 minutes.
3. Once cooked; remove the piecrust from the oven and set aside to cool to room temperature.
4. While the crust is baking, add the flour, salt, vanilla, sugar, sour cream and almond extract to a large bowl.
5. Whisk using a hand whisk or an electric beater until the batter is well combined and has a light creamy texture.
6. Add in the raspberries, strawberries and blackberries.
7. Gently fold making sure that the berries do not get muddled.
8. Pour the prepared mix onto the cooled piecrust and spread evenly. Smooth out the top of the pie using a spatula.
9. Add the Extender Ring to the base.
10. Place the pie on the 1-inch cooking rack.
11. Bake on the 8 power setting for about 40 to 50 minutes or until the pie is well set.
12. One done, place the pie on the cooling rack until cool enough to refrigerate.
13. Refrigerate until chilled before slicing. And Serve chilled.

225. Easy Banana Puddings

Ingredients:
- 3 oz. (90g) butter; melted
- 1/2 cup almond meal
- 3 egg whites
- 3/4 cup icing sugar
- 1/4 cup plain flour
- 0.8 oz. (25g) butter; melted, extra
- 2 tablespoon brown sugar; firmly packed
- 2 medium bananas; sliced thickly

Instructions:
1. Grease four 9.5cm-round 2/3 cup (160ml) ovenproof dishes (I use pie dishes for this).
2. Combine butter, almond meal, egg whites, icing sugar and flour in medium bowl; stir until just combined.

3. Divide extra butter equally among prepared dishes; sprinkle evenly with brown sugar. Divide slices and then pudding mixture equally among dishes.
4. Bake in NuWave oven on 5cm rack for 15mins.
5. When cooked stand puddings 2mins; then run knife around edge and turn out onto serving plates.
6. Serve with custard, cream or ice-cream.

226. Orange Crinkle Cookies

Ingredients:
- 1 cup all-purpose flour
- ¼-teaspoon salt
- 1 teaspoon baking powder
- 3/4 cups granulated sugar; divided
- 1 egg
- 5 tablespoon butter; softened
- Zest from ½ orange
- 2 - 3 drops orange food coloring
- 1 tablespoon orange juice
- ¼-cup powdered sugar
- ½ teaspoon orange extract

Instructions:
1. Sieve together the flour, salt and baking powder together in a medium bowl. Mix well and keep aside.
2. In another bowl place the butter and add in about ½-cup sugar to it. Cream the butter until the sugar is well incorporated.
3. Add the egg to the butter and sugar mix and whisk well until well combined.
4. Pour in the orange juice, orange food color, orange zest and orange extract. Mix well until well combined.
5. Slowly add the flour mix to the wet ingredients in 3 parts, mixing thoroughly after each addition to ensure that there are no lumps.
6. Use a scoop to scoop out about 6 even golf ball sized balls.
7. Empty the granulated sugar into a flat plate and roll the cookie dough balls in the sugar.
8. Sprinkle the powdered sugar over the sugar covered dough balls and place them in a silicon baking ring or a well-greased cookie sheet.
9. Place the baking ring or the cookie sheet on the 1-inch cooking rack.
10. Bake at 350 degrees Fahrenheit for about 12 to 14 minutes or until the edges of the cookies are golden brown.
11. Extract the cookies from the oven and cool them completely before serving.

227. Lemon Candy Topped Iced Cookies

Ingredients to Make the Cookies:
- 2 cups all-purpose flour (sifted)
- 1/2 teaspoon baking powder
- Salt as per taste
- 1/4 cup (1/2 stick) unsalted butter; softened
- 1 cup granulated sugar
- 1/4 cup shortening
- 1 large egg
- 1 teaspoon pure vanilla extract

Ingredients to Make the Icing:
- 1 cup powdered sugar
- 1 – 2 tablespoons milk
- 1/2 teaspoon vanilla
- 1/3 cup crushed lemon candies

Directions to Make the Cookies:
1. Sieve together the flour, salt and baking powder together in a large mixing bowl and keep aside.
2. Place the shortening, sugar, vanilla, butter and egg together in the bowl of an electric mixer.
3. Beat on a low speed until all the ingredients start getting creamed together.
4. Slowly add in the flour mix, a little at a time, to the butter mix.
5. Continue beating until all the flour in incorporated in and forms a smooth dough.
6. Divide the dough into two equal parts.
7. Cover each part of dough in a plastic wrap and refrigerate for about 6 to 8 hours.
8. When you are ready to bake, remove the refrigerated dough from the fridge and leave it out until it reaches room temperature.
9. Place a plastic wrap on your working station and place the dough on it.
10. Cover with another plastic wrap and roll the dough until it is about 1/8-inch thick.
11. Transfer the dough onto a floured working surface. Use a cookie cutter to cut cookies in the shape that you desire.
12. Place the cookies on 1inch intervals on the liner pan.
13. Bake on the '9' setting of your NuWave oven for about 13 to 15 minutes.
14. Once the timer is up, immediately open the dome to release the extra moisture from the oven.
15. Let the cookies cool to a manageable temperature before removing them from the liner pan.
16. Transfer the cookies onto wire rack with parchment paper placed below it.
17. Let the cookies cool completely before glazing them.
18. Repeat with the remaining dough until you have a batch of cookies.

Directions to Make the Icing:
1. Place the milk, powdered sugar and vanilla together in a large bowl.
2. Whisk using a wire whisk and continue beating until the mix is thick enough to spread.
3. Dip the top halves of the cookies into the icing and place them back on the wire rack with the iced side up.
4. You can also fill a piping bag with the icing or use a spoon to drizzle the icing over the cookies.
5. Top with the lemon candies.
6. Serve immediately.

228. NuWave Chocolate Cake

Ingredients:
- ½-cup almond flour
- ½-cup cocoa powder
- ½-cup lentil flour
- ½ teaspoon baking soda
- ¼-cup coconut oil; melted
- ¼-teaspoon salt
- 2 eggs
- 3/8 cup honey
- ¾ teaspoon vanilla

Instructions:
1. Pour a little coconut oil in a 4-inch by 4-inch baking pan. Swirl the pan around until the bottom and the sides are well coated.
2. Sieve together the almond flour, cocoa powder, salt, lentil flour and baking soda together in a large mixing bowl. Keep aside.
3. In another mixing bowl combine the eggs, vanilla, coconut oil and honey together and whisk well until all the ingredients are well incorporated.
4. Pour the almond flour mix into the bowl of a stand mixer.
5. Beat the ingredients with the whisk attachment on the low or medium speed.
6. While whisking, pour the wet ingredients into the bowl gradually. Stop every few minutes to scrape the sides of the bowl.
7. Continue whisking until the volume of the batter doubles.
8. Pour the prepared batter into the greased pan.
9. Place the pan on the 1-inch cooking rack.
10. Add the Extender Rung (3-inch) to the base of your oven.
11. Bake at 325 degrees Fahrenheit for about 35 to 40 minutes or until a knife run through the center of the cake comes out clean.
12. Remove the pan from the oven and cool the cake for about 10 minutes before turning it onto a wire rack. Serve the cake warm.

229. Maraschino Cherry Stuffed Cherry Glazed Cookies

Ingredients to Make the Cookies:
- 3/4 cups flour
- 1/4 cup unsalted butter; softened
- 1/4 teaspoon salt
- 6 tablespoons powdered sugar
- 1/2 teaspoon vanilla
- 1 tablespoon milk
- 12 maraschino cherries; drained from the liquid, liquid reserved for the glaze and stems removed

Ingredients to Make the Glaze:
- 10 tablespoons powdered sugar; divided
- 1 tablespoon reserved maraschino cherry juice
- 1/2 tablespoon butter; melted

Directions to Make the Cookies:
1. Sieve together the flour and salt in a small bowl. Keep aside.
2. Place the butter and sugar together in another bowl and beat with an electronic beater until fluffy and light.
3. Slowly add in the milk; while continuously beating until the milk is incorporated.
4. Add in the vanilla and continue beating.
5. Slowly add in the flour mix in small increments to the butter and milk mixture. Beat until the flour mix is incorporated into the batter to form a smooth dough.
6. Roll the dough into a smooth log and divide it into 12 equal parts.
7. Oil your hands and roll the portions into a small bowl.
8. Lightly press the center of the ball to flatten it.
9. Place a single maraschino cherry in the venter of the dough.
10. Bring the sides of the cookie up and roll the ball until the cherry is completely covered.
11. Place the cherry center balls around the perimeter of a greased liner pan. Leave about an-inch of space between two cookies.
12. Add the Extender Ring to the base of the NuWave oven.
13. Bake on the '9' setting of your NuWave oven for about 20 to 22 minutes.
14. Once the timer is up; immediately open the dome to release the extra moisture from the oven.
15. Let the cookies cool to a manageable temperature before removing them from the liner pan.
16. Transfer the cookies onto wire rack with parchment paper placed below it.
17. Let the cookies cool completely before glazing them.

Directions to Make the Glaze:
1. Place about 8 tablespoons of the powdered sugar, maraschino cherry juice and butter together in a small mixing bowl.
2. Beat on the medium speed with an electronic beater until the glaze is smooth. Add in more maraschino cherry juice if the glaze is too thick.
3. Dip the top halves of the cookies into the glaze and place them back on the wire rack with the glazed side up.
4. You can also fill a piping bag with the glaze or use a spoon to drizzle the glaze over the cookies.
5. Let the glaze set for 15 to 20 minutes and sprinkle the remaining icing sugar over the cookies.
6. Serve immediately.

230. Yummy Apple Crisp

Ingredients:
- 2 fresh apples
- ½-cup sugar
- 3/4 cup all-purpose flour
- ¼-teaspoon salt
- ¼-cup soft butter or margarine
- 1 tablespoon cinnamon
- Whipped cream

Instructions:
1. Scrub and wash the apples well. Peel the apples and thinly slice them.
2. Place the peeled apple slices in the bottom of a 4-inch by 4-inch baking dish. Keep aside.
3. Sieve together the flour, salt, sugar and cinnamon together in a medium sized mixing bowl.
4. Add in the butter and lightly whisk until the mixture resembles coarse sand.
5. Sprinkle the prepared butter and flour mix over the sliced apples.
6. Place the baking pan on the 1-inch cooking rack.
7. Bake at 350 degrees Fahrenheit for about 30 to 45 minutes or until the top crust is brown.
8. Serve warm topped with a dollop of whipped cream.

231. Lemon Cookies Topped With Lemon Candies

Ingredients:
- 2 cups all-purpose flour
- ¼-teaspoon salt
- ¼-cup (½ stick) unsalted butter; softened
- 1 cup granulated sugar
- ½ teaspoon baking powder
- ¼-cup shortening
- 1 teaspoon pure vanilla extract
- 1 large egg

Icing Ingredients:
- 1 cup powdered sugar
- 2 tablespoon milk
- ½ teaspoon vanilla
- 1/3 cup crushed lemon candies

Instructions:
1. Sieve together the flour, salt and baking powder together in a large mixing bowl. Once well combined, keep aside.
2. In another bowl; add in the shortening, sugar, vanilla, butter and egg. Use an electric beater to cream together the ingredients on low speed.
3. Slowly add the flour mix to the butter and egg mix, stopping after each addition to ensure that the flour mix is properly incorporated and there are no lumps.
4. Continue mixing until you get a soft dough.
5. Divide the dough into 4 equal quarters.
6. Wrap each quarter in plastic wrap and refrigerate the dough for 4 to 6 hours or overnight.
7. Before baking, remove the dough from the refrigerator.
8. Leave the dough out until it reaches room temperature.
9. Place the dough between two sheets of plastic wrap and roll until it is about 1/8-inch thick.
10. Lightly dust a working surface with some flour and place the dough on it.
11. Cut the cookies from the sheet using your favorite cookie cutters.
12. Place the cookies on 1-inch intervals on the liner pan.
13. Bake at 300 degrees Fahrenheit for about 14 to 16 minutes or until the edges of the cookies start browning.
14. Rest the cookies in the liner pan for a few minutes before transferring the cookies to a cooling rack.

15. Repeat the steps from 7 to 14 to prepare the remaining cookies.
16. Make sure you cool the cookies completely before icing them.

Icing Instructions:
1. Combine the powdered sugar, milk and vanilla together in a large mixing bowl.
2. Mix until the icing has the consistency of a spread.
3. Pour the prepared icing over the cooled cookies.
4. Serve topped with the lemon candies.

232. Raspberry Crumble

Ingredients:
- 2 tablespoon unsalted butter; softened
- ¼-cup all-purpose flour
- 3/8 cup brown sugar
- ½ pint fresh raspberries
- 1 tablespoon cornstarch
- ¼-cup sugar
- ½ lemon; juiced

Instructions:
1. Place the butter, flour and brown sugar in a medium sized mixing bowl.
2. Mix the ingredients together using your hands, until the mixture resembles coarse sand. Keep aside.
3. In another mixing bowl; mix together the raspberries, cornstarch, sugar and lemon juice.
4. Pour the prepared raspberry filling into a greased ramekin and smooth out the top of the filling using a rubber coated spatula.
5. Sprinkle the prepared crumb topping over the raspberry filling.
6. Place the ramekin on the 2-inch cooking rack.
7. Add the Extender Ring to the base if required.
8. Bake on the 8 power setting for about 18 to 22 minutes or until the top crumb layer is golden brown.
9. Cool slightly and serve it warm.

233. Tasty Carrot Cake Cookies

For: 24 cookies

Ingredients:
- 1/4 cup packed light-brown sugar
- 1/4 cup sugar
- 1/4 cup oil
- 1/4 cup applesauce or fruit puree
- 1 eggs
- 1/2 teaspoon vanilla
- 1/2 cup flour
- 1/2 cup whole wheat flour
- 1/2 teaspoon baking soda
- 1/2 teaspoon baking powder
- 1/8 teaspoon salt
- 1/2 teaspoon ground cinnamon
- 1/4 teaspoon ground nutmeg
- 1/4 teaspoon ground ginger
- 1 cups old-fashioned rolled oats (raw)
- 3/4 cup finely grated carrots (about 2 carrots)
- 1/2 cup raisins or golden raisins

Instructions:
1. Mix together sugars, oil, applesauce, egg, and vanilla.
2. In a separate bowl; mix together all dry ingredients.
3. Add dry ingredients into wet ingredients. Mix until just blended. Stir in carrots and raisins.
4. Drop by teaspoonful onto silicone baking ring or parchment-lined cookie sheet.
5. Place on 1-inch rack and cook at 300 degrees F (Level 8) for 12-14 minutes or until golden brown. Serve warm.

234. Tasty Banana Bread

Ingredients:
- 5 very ripe bananas (6 if they are smaller ones)
- 3/4 cup white sugar
- 1 teaspoon. vanilla
- 2 cups plain flour
- 1 teaspoon baking powder
- 1 teaspoon baking soda
- 1 teaspoon ground cinnamon

Instructions:
1. Mash the bananas until smooth. Add sugar and vanilla and blend well.
2. In another bowl; mix the sifted dry ingredients until well blended and add to the bananas.
3. Bake in NuWave oven; on 5cm rack, power level 8, in a greased loaf pan for 45-50 minutes.

235. Chocolate Tart

Ingredients:
- 1 cup crushed sea salt potato chips
- 3 tablespoons melted unsalted butter
- 2 tablespoons all-purpose flour
- 10 tablespoons heavy cream; divided
- 1/2 teaspoon vanilla extract
- 5 ounces semisweet chocolate morsels
- ¼ teaspoon salt
- 4 ounces bittersweet chocolate morsels
- 1 large egg
- Sea salt for garnish

Instructions:
1. Place the crushed sea salt flavored potato chips, flour and melted butter together in the jar of a blender or food processor. Blitz for about a minute until all the ingredients are well combined.
2. Lightly grease a spring form pan with some butter or spray with some cooking spray.
3. Press the prepared chip and melted butter mixture in the bottom and over the sides of the greased spring form pan.
4. Place the spring form pan on a 3-inch rack and bake on the 'HI' setting for about 5 minutes until the crust hardens.
5. Remove the crust from the oven and keep aside until cooled to room temperature.
6. Pour about 2 tablespoons of the heavy whipping cream into a small saucepan. Heat over a medium low flame until the heavy cream is just lightly bubbling.
7. Reduce the flame to a low and add the semisweet chocolate morsels to the cream. Gently mix using a rubber spatula until the chocolate melts and becomes smooth. Take off heat.

8. Add in the salt and vanilla to the chocolate mix. Mix well.
9. Add the eggs one by one to the chocolate mix and mix well until the egg is incorporated, before adding another egg.
10. Pour the prepared salted chocolate mix onto the prepared crust and tap lightly against the kitchen counter to ensure that there are no air bubbles.
11. Place the Extender Ring on the base of your NuWave oven and place the spring form pan on the 1-inch rack.
12. Bake on the '8' setting for about 16 to 18 minutes.
13. Increase the temperature setting to '9' and bake for another 10 minutes.
14. Remove the pan from the oven and cool for a few minutes.
15. While the pie cools, prepare the ganache.
16. Heat the remaining heavy whipping cream on a medium high flame in a saucepan until lightly bubbling.
17. Take the saucepan off the heat and add the bittersweet chocolate morsels to the warm cream. Mix well until smooth.
18. Once the pie is cooled; pour the prepared ganache over it. Use a spatula to make an even layer.
19. Refrigerate for 8 to 10 hours or until overnight.
20. Cut into slices and serve topped with a pinch of sea salt.

236. Oatmeal Cookie Cake

Ingredients:
- 3/4 cup all-purpose flour
- ½ teaspoon ground cinnamon
- ½ teaspoon baking soda
- ¼-teaspoon salt
- 1 tablespoon cornstarch
- 1/8 teaspoon nutmeg
- ½-cup margarine or butter; softened
- ¼-cup granulated sugar
- 6 tablespoon firmly packed brown sugar
- ½ egg
- ½-cup golden raisins
- ½ teaspoon vanilla
- 1 ½-cups old fashioned rolled oats
- Frosting; optional

Instructions:
1. Sieve together the flour, cinnamon, nutmeg, baking soda, salt and cornstarch together in a small mixing bowl. Mix well until well combined. Keep aside.
2. In the bowl of a stand mixer, place the margarine. Add in the granulated sugar and the brown sugar and whisk on the low speed until the butter is fluffy and light.
3. Add in the egg and vanilla and continue beating until all the ingredients are incorporated.
4. Slowly add in the previously sieved dry ingredients and beat well until you get a smooth and lump free dough.
5. Slowly add in the oats and raisins and mix well until incorporated.
6. Lightly grease a silicone pizza liner with some butter and press the dough into the bottom of the greased silicone pan.

7. Add the Extender Ring to the base of the oven.
8. Bake the cookie cake at 350 degrees Fahrenheit for about 22 to 25 minutes.
9. Extract the cookie cake from the oven and cool for a few minutes before flipping it onto a 3-inch cooking rack.
10. Carefully peel the liner pan of it.
11. Return the cookie cake to the oven and bake for about 15 to 17 minutes at 300 degrees Fahrenheit.
12. Once done; cool the cookie cake and cover with the frosting of your choice if you want. And Serve immediately.

237. Pear Custard Pie

Ingredients:
- 1 ½ pears, peeled; halved, sliced into ¼-inch pieces
- 1/8 cup unsalted butter; melted
- 1/8 teaspoon nutmeg; plus extra for dusting
- 1/6 cup granulated sugar
- 1 teaspoon vanilla extract
- 1/6 cup all-purpose flour
- 1 ½ large eggs
- 1/8 teaspoon salt
- ½-cup milk
- Butter or non-stick cooking spray

Optional Ingredients:
- Confectioners' sugar

Instructions:
1. Grease the sides and the bottom of a 5-inch tart pan with the nonstick cooking spray or with butter.
2. Place the pear slices in a spiral in the greased tart pan, beginning from the outside and slowly working towards the center.
3. Sprinkle the nutmeg over the pears and keep the tart pan aside.
4. Place the butter, flour, eggs, salt, sugar, vanilla, salt and milk together in the jar of a blender.
5. Blitz for about 30 to 45 seconds or until the batter has a smooth consistency.
6. Pour the prepared custard over the pears.
7. Place the tart pan on the 2-inch cooking rack.
8. Add the Extender Ring to the base of the oven.
9. Bake on the HI power setting for about 35 to 40 minutes or until the custard is set.
10. Transfer the pie to a cooling rack and cool until just warm.
11. Flip the pie over to a serving plate and serve warm or chill before serving.

238. Delicious Jam Biscuits and Almond

Ingredients:
- 4.5 oz. (125g) unsalted butter
- 1/2 cup caster sugar
- 1-2 teaspoon grated orange zest
- 2 eggs
- 1 teaspoon vanilla extract
- pinch salt

- 1 cup plain flour
- 1/2 cup almond meal
- 1 cup slivered almonds; chopped
- 3/4 cup raspberry or any favourite jam

Instructions:
1. Beat together butter, sugar and orange zest until light and creamy. Add eggs one at a time.
2. Stir through vanilla and pinch salt.
3. Fold through sifted flour and almond meal; knead until you get smooth, light dough.
4. Roll into 2 teaspoonoonful-sized balls and roll in the slivered almonds, pressing lightly to get them to stick to the dough. Flatten slightly and make an indentation in the middle of each biscuit and fill with jam.
5. Bake on baking paper on 5cm rack in NuWave oven (add extender ring) for 18mins.
6. Allow to cool 5mins on paper before transferring to cooling rack.

239. Amazing Scones

Ingredients:
- 2 1/2 cups self raising flour
- 1 teaspoon salt
- 1/4 cup cream
- 1 teaspoon vanilla extract
- 1 cup lemonade (fresh)

Instructions:
1. Sift flour and salt into a medium bowl.
2. Make well in center of flour and add cream, vanilla & lemonade.
3. Cut through mixture with a knife until mixed.
4. Turn out sticky dough mixture onto lightly floured bench or pastry sheet, sprinkle lightly with flour and gently knead dough until smooth.
5. Pat down to about 3cm (1") high and cut scones with a 5cm (2") round cutter.
6. Lightly spray bottom of pan (that comes with your extender kit) or a small flat tray with spray oil.
7. Place scones in pan about 1cm-2cm apart and brush tops with milk.
8. Bake in NuWave oven on 5cm rack (that comes with your extender kit) for 10-12 mins on level 10 – there is no need to set this level as your NuWave will default to this setting automatically. I like to turn my scones over for the last 2 minutes but this is not necessary!
9. Remove from oven and allow to cool on rack.

240. Easy Honey Cornbread

Ingredients:
- 1 cup all-purpose flour
- 1 cup yellow cornmeal
- ¼ cup white sugar
- 1 tablespoon baking powder
- 1 cup heavy cream
- ¼ cup vegetable oil
- ¼ cup honey
- 2 eggs; lightly beaten

Instructions:
1. Lightly grease 10 x 10 baking pan.

2. In a large mixing bowl; stir together flour, cornmeal, sugar, and baking powder. Add in cream, oil, honey, and eggs. Stir to combine.
3. Pour into baking pan. Bake on 1-inch rack on Power Level High (350 degrees F) for 20 minutes. Let rest for 1-2 minutes before removing from NuWave Oven.

241. Coconut Slice and Raspberry

Ingredients:
- 1 cup plain flour
- 2.3 oz. (65g) butter; chopped coarsely
- 1 egg yolk
- 2 tablespoon water; approximately
- 1/4 cup raspberry jam
- 1 cup desiccated coconut
- 1 egg; beaten lightly
- 1/4 cup caster sugar

Instructions:
1. Place flour in a medium bowl; rub in butter using fingertips. Add egg yolk and enough of the water to make a firm dough when ingredients are pressed together using hands.
2. Turn dough onto a lightly floured surface, knead gently until smooth. Place dough into a 20cm x 20cm greased pan. Use a glass to roll dough evenly over base of pan (or use fingertips).
3. Bake in NuWave oven; on 5cm rack, for 20mins or until browned lightly; stand for 10min.
4. Spread jam evenly over pastry.
5. Combine coconut, egg and sugar in medium bowl; mix using fork until all the coconut is moist. Spread coconut mixture over jam; do not flatten.
6. Bake in NuWave oven on 5cm rack for 8 minutes until golden brown. Allow to cool in pan. Cut into squares.

242. Ginger Anzac and Macadamia Biscuits

Ingredients:
- 4.5 oz. (125g) butter
- 2 tablespoons golden syrup
- 1/2 teaspoon bicarbonate of soda
- 2 tablespoon boiling water
- 1 cup (90g) rolled oats
- 1cup (150g) plain flour
- 1 cup (220g) firmly packed brown sugar
- 3/4 cup (60g) desiccated coconut
- 1/2 cup (65g) finely chopped macadamias
- 1/4 cup (45g) finely chopped glace ginger

Instructions:
1. Combine oats, flour, sugar, coconut, macadamias and ginger in a large bowl.
2. Mix butter and golden syrup in a small saucepan over a low heat until smooth.
3. Stir in combined bi-carb soda and water and pour mixture over dry ingredients.
4. Roll level tablespoons of mixture into balls, slightly flatten with a fork when placing on a piece of baking paper (about 5cm apart) on 5cm rack of NuWave oven.
5. Bake on power level 8 for 15 minutes.
6. Cool on cooling rack.

243. Cheesecake Cookies

Ingredients:
- 1 3/4 cups all-purpose flour
- A pinch of salt
- 1 (8 ounce) package cream cheese; softened
- 1 teaspoon baking powder
- 3/4 cups sugar
- 1 ¼-cups butter; softened
- 1 large egg
- ½ tablespoon orange liqueur
- ½-cup confectioners' sugar
- 1 teaspoon vanilla extract
- ½-cup graham cracker crumbs
- 1 (20 ounce) can cherry pie filling

Instructions:
1. Sieve together the flour, salt and baking powder in a small mixing bowl. Keep aside.
2. In another bowl; place the cream cheese, sugar and butter together. Beat with an electric mixer for about 2 minutes or until the mix is creamy, fluffy and smooth.
3. Slowly add in the egg, orange liqueur and vanilla extract to the bowl. Continue whisking until well incorporated.
4. Gradually add in the confectioners' sugar and mix well until all the sugar is well incorporated.
5. Slowly add the prepared dry ingredient mix to the bowl and continue whisking until the ingredients are just combined. Do not over mix.
6. Cover the dough with a plastic wrap and refrigerate for about 45 minutes or until the dough is firm to touch.
7. Place a silicone baking ring on the 2 inch cooking rack.
8. In a wide and shallow dish add in the graham cracker crumbs.
9. Roll the chilled dough into 1-inch balls and then dredge the balls through the graham cracker crumbs until well coated.
10. Place the graham cracker crumb coated dough balls in the silicone baking ring, leaving about ½ inch space between 2 balls.
11. Lightly press the center of each dough ball.
12. Bake on the HI power setting for about 10 to 12 minutes.
13. Open the dome of the oven and carefully place about 3 cherries in the indentation on each cookie.
14. Close the dome and continue baking on the HI power setting for another 3 to 4 minutes or until the cherries are set.
15. Remove the rack from the oven and cool the cookies completely before serving.

244. Tasty Salted Chocolate Tart

Ingredients:
- 1 cup crushed sea salt potato chips
- 1/8 cup all-purpose flour
- 2 ½ tablespoon unsalted butter; melted
- 5/8 cup heavy cream; divided
- ½ teaspoon vanilla extract
- 5 - oz. semisweet chocolate morsels

- 1/8 teaspoon salt
- 4 - oz. bittersweet chocolate morsels
- 1 large egg
- Sea salt for garnish

Instructions:
1. Place the crushed sea salt potato chips, flour and melted butter together in the jar of a food processor. Blitz for about 30 to 45 seconds or until all the ingredients are well combined.
2. Transfer the prepared mix into a 5-inch springform pan and press it gently into the bottom and the sides of the pan.
3. Place the pan on the 4-inch cooking rack and bake on the HI power setting for about 5 to 7 minutes or until the crust is set. Keep it aside to cool.
4. Add about 2 tablespoon of the heavy cream to a small saucepan and heat over a medium low flame until the heavy cream is lightly bubbling.
5. Reduce the flame to low and add the semisweet chocolate morsels to the pan.
6. Stir constantly using a rubber spatula until the mixture is smooth and well combined.
7. Add in the salt and vanilla to the chocolate and cream mixture and mix well until well combined.
8. Add in the egg and stir well until the egg is well incorporated.
9. Pour the prepared chocolate mixture on the cool crust and smoothen the top using a spatula.
10. Place the Extender Ring on the base of the oven.
11. Place the pan on the 1-inch cooking rack.
12. Bake on the 8 power setting for about 15 to 17 minutes
13. Increase the power setting to the 9 power setting and bake for an additional 8 to 10 minutes or until the chocolate mixture is set.
14. Remove the pan from the oven and set aside to cool
15. Prepare the ganache by pouring the remaining heavy cream into a small saucepan.
16. Heat the heavy cream on a medium low flame until the cream is lightly bubbling.
17. Reduce the heat to a low and add in the bittersweet chocolate morsels.
18. Stir continuously until the chocolate and the cream is well combine and the mixture is smooth.
19. Pour the prepared ganache over the cooled pie and use a spatula to spread it into an even layer.
20. Refrigerate the pie 4 to 6 hours or overnight.
21. Slice into pieces and serve topped with a pinch of coarse sea salt.

245. Tasty Butter Biscuits

Makes 50-60

Ingredients:
- 6 oz. (175g) soft unsalted butter
- 1 teaspoon baking powder
- 7 oz. (200g) caster sugar
- 1 teaspoon salt
- 2 large eggs
- 10.5 oz. (300g) icing sugar, sieved and food coloring

- 14 oz. (400g) plain flour (plus more if needed)

Required:
- Biscuit cutters
- 2 baking sheets greased or lined

Instructions:
1. Cream the butter and sugar together until pale and moving towards mousiness, then beat in the eggs and vanilla.
2. In another bowl; combine the flour, baking powder and salt. Add the dry ingredients to the butter and egg. Mix gently but surely. If the mixture is too sticky to be rolled out, add more flour but do so sparingly as too much will make the dough tough.
3. Halve the dough; make them into fat discs, wrap each half in clingwrap and rest in the fridge for a least 1hour.
4. Sprinkle a suitable surface with flour, place a disc of dough on it (don't take the other half out of the fridge until finished with the first). Sprinkle a little more flour on top of the disc.
5. Roll it out to a thickness of about 1/2cm.
6. Cut into shape, (dipping the cutter into flour as you go) place the biscuits a little apart on the baking sheets.
7. Bake in NuWave oven on 5cm rack; for 8-10 minutes, by which time they will be lightly golden around the edges.
8. Cool on a rack and continue with the remaining dough.
9. When they are completely cooled; you can get on with the icing.
10. Put a couple of tablespoons of almost boiling water into a large bowl. Add the sieved icing sugar and mix together; adding more water as you need to form a thick paste. Colour and decorate as desired.

246. Stuffed Baked Apples

Ingredients:
- 4 large apples; (Honeycrisp, Fuji, Rome)
- ¼ cup coconut flakes
- ¼ cup dried cranberries or apricots
- 2 teaspoons orange zest; grated
- 1/2 cup orange juice
- 2 tablespoons brown sugar
- 1/2 cup chopped pecans

Instructions:
1. Cut top off apple and hollow out center with knife or apple corer. Arrange in non-stick baking pan.
2. In a bowl; combine coconut, cranberries, and orange zest. Divide evenly and fill centers of apples.
3. In a bowl; mix orange juice and brown sugar. Pour over apples.
4. Place pan on 1-inch rack and cook 5-6 minutes until apples are tender. Serve warm.

247. Halloween Special Pumpkin Cheesecake

Ingredients:

- ½-cup granulated sugar
- ½ tablespoon all-purpose flour
- ½ teaspoon confectioners' sugar
- Pinch of ground cloves
- ¼-teaspoon ground cinnamon
- Pinch of ground nutmeg
- 1 (8 ounce) package cream cheese; softened
- 1 egg at room temperature
- ¼-cup canned pumpkin puree
- 1 (3 ounce) ready to use graham cracker crust
- ¼-teaspoon vanilla

Instructions:

1. Combine the granulated sugar, confectioner's sugar, flour, ground cloves, ground nutmeg and ground cinnamon together in a small mixing bowl. Keep aside.
2. Place the cream cheese in a large mixing bowl. Add in the pumpkin puree and whisk well until well combined.
3. Pour the prepared flour and sugar mixture into the cream cheese mixture and mix well until well combined.
4. Add the eggs to the flour and margarine mixture one at a time, whisking well after each addition to ensure that the eggs are well incorporated.
5. Pour in the vanilla and whisk until well combined.
6. Pour the filling onto the ready to use graham cracker crust.
7. Place the filled crust on the 2-inch cooking rack.
8. Add the Extender Ring to the base of the oven.
9. Bake the prepared cheesecake at 300 degrees Fahrenheit for about 40 to 45 minutes.
10. Place the cheesecake on the cooling rack.
11. When the bottom of the cheesecake is cool enough to touch, transfer the cheesecake to the refrigerator and cool for about 6 to 8 hours or overnight.
12. Slice the cheesecake into desired pieces and serve.

248. Maple Glazed Dense Pound Cake

Ingredients:
Cake Ingredients:

- ½ pound butter; softened
- 3 large eggs
- 1 ½-cups sugar
- 2 cups flour
- 1 teaspoon vanilla extract
- ½-cup milk

Maple Glaze Ingredients:

- 2 tablespoon milk
- ½-cup powdered sugar
- 2 tablespoon maple syrup

Instructions:

1. Place the butter in a large mixing bowl. Gradually add the sugar to it and cream well until the butter is smooth and creamy.

2. Add in the eggs and whisk until just combined. Add the eggs one at a time, whisking well after each addition to ensure that the egg is well incorporated.
3. Sieve the flour into the egg mixture and mix well until just combined.
4. Pour in the vanilla extract and the milk and mix well until it forms a smooth and uniformly thick batter.
5. Pour the prepared batter into a loaf pan or a 4-inch by 4-inch baking pan.
6. Place the loaf pan on the 1-inch cooking rack and bake at 3000 degrees Fahrenheit for about 50 to 60 minutes.
7. While the cake bakes, prepare the glaze.
8. Pour the milk in a small mixing bowl.
9. Add in the maple syrup and powdered sugar.
10. Whisk well until it gets a smooth glaze like consistency.
11. Once the cake is done; cool in the pan for a few minutes before inverting the cake onto a cooling rack.
12. Slice the cake and pour the prepared glaze over it. And Serve warm.

249. Egg-Less Arrowroot Biscuits

Ingredients:
- 1/3 cup arrowroot
- 1 cup plain flour/all-purpose flour
- 1/2 teaspoon baking powder
- 3 oz. (90g) butter
- 1/4 cup soft brown sugar
- 2 tablespoon milk (approx.)
- pinch of salt

Instructions:
1. Sift the dry ingredients into a bowl; rub in the butter until the mixture is like fine breadcrumbs.
2. Add the sugar and milk to mix to a stiff dough.
3. Turn on to a floured surface and roll until very thin, prick all over with a fork and cut into approx. 5cm (2") rounds or ovals. Refrigerate dough to firm if it becomes too soft to handle.
4. Place on baking paper on 5cm rack and bake in NuWave oven for 10-15 minutes or until golden brown; turn and cook for another 5 minutes. Cool on wire racks.

TIP: Make sure baking paper is long enough to be captured by both sides of the dome when put on – this will ensure the paper does not get blown onto the biscuits by the convection during cooking!

250. Orange and Buttermilk Cupcakes

Ingredients:

Cupcake Ingredients:
- 3/4 cups flour
- Pinch of salt
- 3/8 teaspoon baking soda
- 3 tablespoon unsalted butter
- ½ teaspoon vanilla extract
- ½-cup sugar
- ¼-teaspoon orange extract
- 3/8 cup buttermilk
- 1 egg; room temperature

Orange Cream Frosting Ingredients:
- ½ (8 ounce) package cream cheese; room temperature
- 1 cup powdered sugar
- 2 tablespoon butter; room temperature
- 1 tablespoon orange extract
- ½ tablespoon vanilla extract

Optional Ingredients:
- Orange food coloring

Instructions:

Instructions for Cupcake:
1. Sieve together the flour, salt and baking soda together in a small mixing bowl. Keep aside.
2. Place the butter in a medium pot and heat over a low flame until the butter has melted.
3. Add in the sugar and continue heating for about 1 minute, stirring constantly.
4. Take the pot off heat and add in the vanilla extract, orange extract and egg.
5. Mix well until well combined.
6. Gradually add the flour mix and the buttermilk alternatingly to the pan, starting and ending with the dry ingredients. Stir well after each addition to ensure there are no lumps.
7. Pour the prepared batter into 6 cupcake liners.
8. Place the prepared cupcakes on the 2-inch cooking rack.
9. Add the Extender Ring to the base of the oven.
10. Bake on the 8-power setting for about 13 to 16 minutes or until a knife run through the center of the cupcake comes out clean.
11. Open the dome of the oven and carefully remove the rack from the oven.
12. Cool the cupcakes for 5 to 7 minutes before removing the liners from the cupcakes.

Instructions for Frosting:
1. While the cupcakes cook; place the cream cheese and butter in the bowl of a stand mixer.
2. Beat slowly on the low speed until the butter and cream cheese are well mixed.
3. Slowly add in the confectioners' sugar, while constantly beating on the low speed, until all the sugar is well incorporated.
4. Add in the vanilla extract; orange food coloring and orange extract to the bowl. Continue whisking until well blended.
5. Spoon or pipe the prepared frosting over the cooled cupcakes.
6. Serve topped with some orange candy or sprinkles.

Made in the USA
Lexington, KY
05 May 2019